What Would Jesus Do Now?

Wes Neal

＃ *what Would* **Jesus** *Do Now?*

Wes Neal

WHAT WOULD JESUS DO NOW?

Wes Neal, What Would Jesus Do Now?

ISBN 1-887002-67-7

Cross Training Publishing
P.O. Box 1541
Grand Island, NE 68802
(308) 384-5762

Copyright © 1997 by Cross Training Publishing

All rights reserved. No part of this book may be reproduced without written permission from the publisher, except by a reviewer who may quote brief passages in a review; nor may any part of this book be reproduced, stored in a retrieval system or transmitted in any form or other without written permission from the publisher.

This book is manufactured in the United States of America.

Library of Congress Cataloging in Publication Data in Progress.

Published by Cross Training Publishing,
P.O. Box 1541
Grand Island, NE 68802
1-800-430-8588

I DEDICATE THIS BOOK

To My Wife

When I married you, I married the best! You're my closest friend, you know. How fortunate is the man who can say his wife is both his lover and closest friend -- and mean it. I can! And, Peggy, your encouragement, insights and suggestions, as we worked through the manuscript for this book together, are forever interwoven in its pages. It's a book written by both of us. Thanks for playing such a big part in making it readable. I love you!

And to My Mother

How I appreciate the example of Christ-likeness you showed Carrie and me as we grew up. I remember the days you'd drop what you were doing to take me to the ball park before I could drive. Days? I mean years! The way you sacrificed what you wanted to do for the sake of your two kids is still a clear example in my mind of Christ-like giving. For your love and care in bringing the two of us up after Dad died, I'll always be grateful. I love you!

SPECIAL ACKNOWLEDGEMENTS

* To Bruce Day for his outstanding cartoons illustrating major points in this book.

* To Steve Joannes, Ruth Milam, Dan Roberts and Jean Smith, who together put in over 300 man hours in working through the manuscripts several times, adding insights, and most of all, adding their fantastic Christ-like enthusiasm in making it possible to get this message to the Christian world!

TABLE OF CONTENTS

Part One — Foundation For The Christian Life

Chapter 1 — What, Another Book? 1

Chapter 2 — Why Should I Do As Jesus Would Do? 5

Chapter 3 — The First Step 11

Chapter 4 — Now, That's What I Call A Goal! 21

Chapter 5 — Hey, Cheer Up, You're Really Loved! 33

Chapter 6 — Love Produces Action 43

Chapter 7 — Your Incredible Partnership 51

Part Two — Biblical Handles For Living The Christian Life

Chapter 8 — The Five "S" Mental Approach 63

Chapter 9 — Focal Points 75

Chapter 10 — Visualizing Your Real Audience 81

Part Three — Getting To Know Jesus Better

Chapter 11 — Looking For What Benefits Others 85

Chapter 12 — Giving Up Your Right To Be Appreciated 89

Chapter 13 — How To Meet A New Day 93

Chapter 14 — Safeguarding Priorities 97

Chapter 15 — How To Be More Effective 103

Chapter 16 — Show No Partiality 107

Chapter 17 — Seeing Someone's Potential 111

Chapter 18 — Handling Pressure On Your Convictions 115

Chapter 19 — Having Empathy 119

Chapter 20 — No Odds Against God's Results 123

Chapter 21 — Exposing Another Person's
              Weakness 127

Chapter 22 — Curbing Your Anger 133

Chapter 23 — Asking For Encouragement 137

Chapter 24 — What To Do When A Friend Lets
              You Down 141

Chapter 25 — Handling Differences With A Leader 145

**Part Four — Practical How To's For Living The
              Christian Life**

Chapter 26 — What To Do When You Don't Know
              What To Do 149

Chapter 27 — But, I Don't Want To Do What
              Jesus Would Do 155

Chapter 28 — Establishing Christ-Like Objectives
              And Scheduling 159

Chapter 29 — Developing Willpower 171

Chapter 30 — Preparing For The Day 181

Part Five — In Conclusion

Chapter 31 — One Last Word 187

Part Six — Tear-Outs

"...FIXING OUR EYES ON JESUS, THE AUTHOR AND PERFECTER OF FAITH..."

Hebrews 12:2

PART ONE

FOUNDATION FOR THE CHRISTIAN LIFE

CHAPTER ONE

WHAT, ANOTHER BOOK?

One day, while visiting a friend in Phoenix, I noticed a large box of books in his car. When I asked what the books were, he reached in and handed me one. "Here," he said. "You must have read it already, haven't you?" He placed IN HIS STEPS by Charles Sheldon in my hand. I looked at it and remarked I hadn't read it. "That's unbelievable!" he said. "You teach exactly the same things this book talks about. You both emphasize that our only goal should be to become Christ-like."

"Well, that's easy to explain," I replied. "That's one of the major themes of the Bible!" I went on to share with my friend that I believed God will continue to make Christ-likeness a major theme in the years to come just as He had in past years.

I took IN HIS STEPS home, and my wife and I eagerly read through its pages. It's a novel about men and women in the late 1800s who made a commitment to ask what Jesus would do before they made any major decision. The book relates how their commitment changed their own lives and influenced the lives of people around them. As my wife and I finished reading it, we weren't surprised to find out it had been a best-selling novel among Christian books for over a half century.

HOW DO YOU FOLLOW IN HIS STEPS?

But, although IN HIS STEPS has been around for many years with its challenge to Christ-likeness, **we Christians still find it difficult to know how to follow in His steps, don't we?** That's why I've written this book. How do you follow in the steps of Jesus? How do you know what He'd do in your particular situations? I've written this book with these questions in mind.

The greatest challenge ever given a Christian is to follow Jesus Christ. When we're following Him, we're following God! And, God made it possible for us to follow Him. He didn't just shout from heaven, "Do things My way!" But, He sent His Son to show us how to do things His way, as well as pay the penalty for our sins. And, not only did God give us Jesus Christ as our example to follow, but He also gave us the Holy Spirit to empower us to live His way. **So, following in the steps of Jesus is possible. We have Jesus as our example of Christ-likeness and the Holy Spirit's power to be Christ-like.**

IT'S A WIDESPREAD PROBLEM

When I first began to ponder what Jesus would do in my various situations, I must have fallen short of knowing what He'd do at least 80% of the time. And, I had been a Christian for over 12 years! In the beginning, I'd ask myself what Jesus would do in handling a flat tire or interruptions from other people. I'd ask what balance He'd have between having time for Himself as well as having time for His family if He had one. I'd ask what things would be a priority in His daily schedule if He were in my place. But I came up short in really knowing how Jesus would handle these situations.

Since then, I've talked to Christians throughout the country and I've discovered my experience wasn't unusual. I've come to realize this is a wide-spread problem, and the reasons are many. But one reason seems to stand above the rest. It's difficult to know what Jesus would do in our situations because we haven't really gotten to know Him. And, if we don't know what He'd do, we can't follow in His steps. **One of the purposes of this book is to help you more intimately get to know Jesus Christ and His way of doing things.**

YOUR GREATEST CHALLENGE AND ADVENTURE

Yes, we'll have failures in following the example of Jesus, but remember, we have living within us the Holy Spirit. The Holy Spirit's power is tapped in the believer when we understand what God wants us to think and do and commit our will to do it. He's our Helper in becoming Christ-like.

Pondering what Jesus would do throughout the day is the **greatest mental challenge** you'll ever face. Then, committing yourself to have His attitudes, thoughts and actions, as the Holy Spirit empowers you, will become your **greatest adventure!** Read on, and we'll see how it's done.

FOR INDEPENDENT AND GROUP STUDY

1. Why do you think Jesus spent over three years in a teaching ministry, instead of going right to the cross to pay the penalty for our sins?

2. Why would pondering what Jesus would do in each of your situations be such a great mental challenge?

3. What are some situations in your life where you'd like to know what Jesus would do, but don't know at the present time?

"LET THE WORD OF CHRIST RICHLY DWELL WITHIN YOU, WITH ALL WISDOM TEACHING AND ADMONISHING ONE ANOTHER WITH PSALMS AND HYMNS AND SPIRITUAL SONGS, SINGING WITH THANKFULNESS IN YOUR HEARTS TO GOD."

Colossians 3:16

CHAPTER TWO

WHY SHOULD I DO AS JESUS WOULD DO?

Why follow Jesus when I can do my own thing?

Why should we pattern our lives after Jesus? After all, since the Bible also talks a lot about God the Father and God the Holy Spirit, what makes Jesus so important? In this chapter we'll look at answers to these questions. If we're going to consider what Jesus would do in each of our situations, it's important we know why all of our efforts should be put into patterning our lives after Him and His way of doing things. Let's consider four facts the Bible teaches concerning Jesus Christ.

Fact One. God's word tells us that Jesus Christ is the God of the Old Testament.

1. In fact, Jesus Christ is the **central figure** of the Old Testament. Over 300 prophecies in the Old Testament pointed to the coming Messiah. **And, Jesus fulfilled them all!** Now, what are the chances any one man could fulfill all of the Old Testament prophecies concerning the Messiah?

Josh McDowell, author of the best selling book, EVIDENCE THAT DEMANDS A VERDICT, includes in his book some astonishing facts Professor Peter Stoner gave in an article in Science Speaks (Moody Press, 1963). They concerned the odds against any one man fulfilling **only eight selected prophecies** concerning the Messiah. The prophecies Professor Stoner selected were the Messiah's place of birth (Micah 5:2), being preceded by a messenger (Isaiah 40:3), entering Jerusalem on a donkey (Zechariah 9:9), being betrayed by a friend (Psalms 41:9), being betrayed for 30 pieces of silver (Zechariah 11:12), the money then being thrown into God's House and being used to buy a potter's field (Zechariah 11:13), the Messiah being silent before His accusers (Isaiah 53:7) and His hands and feet being pierced as He would be crucified with thieves (Psalms 22:16 and Isaiah 53:12).

Professor Stoner concluded the chance any one man would have in fulfilling all eight of these prophecies would be **1 in 100,000,000,000,000,000!** That's a bundle, isn't it? He then went on to illustrate the staggering improbability of that happening outside of God's direct planning. He used the illustration of that incredible number of silver dollars being dumped onto the state of Texas with one of the dollars being marked for identification purposes. Using mathematical calculations he said Texas would then be **two feet deep with silver dollars from border to border.** A blindfolded man would then be told to travel as far as he wanted throughout the state and randomly try to select the only marked silver dollar **on his first try.** Professor Stoner said the calculated chance the blindfolded man would have in picking the marked silver dollar, on his first try, would be the same chance all eight selected prophecies would have in coming true in one man outside of God's intervention. Over 300 Messianic prophecies, all fulfilled in Jesus of Nazareth, is overwhelming proof that Jesus is God's Anointed One.

2. "I AM" is how the God of the Old Testament described Himself (Exodus 3:14). Jesus used these same words to describe Himself.

"Jesus said to them, 'Truly, truly, I say to you, before Abraham was born, **I AM**' "

John 8:58

Fact Two. Jesus made the world.

"All things **came into being through Him;** and apart from Him nothing came into being that has come into being."

John 1:3

"For in Him all things were created, both in the heavens and on earth, visible and invisible, whether thrones or dominions or rulers or authorities -- all things have been created through Him and for Him. And He is before all things, and **in Him all things hold together."**

Colossians 1:16-17

"God, after He spoke long ago to the fathers in the prophets in many portions and in many ways, in these last days has spoken to us in His Son, whom He appointed heir of all things, **through whom also He made the world."**

Hebrews 1:1-2

Fact Three. Jesus is the physical revelation of the invisible God.

"And He is **the image of the invisible God,** the first born of all creation."

Colossians 1:15

"And the Word became flesh, and dwelt among us, and we beheld His glory, glory as of the only begotten from the Father, full of grace and truth."

John 1:14

"No man has seen God at anytime; the only begotten God [Son], who is in the bosom of the Father, **He has explained Him.**"

John 1:18

Fact Four. Jesus Christ claimed total equality with God the Father and with God the Holy Spirit.

1. He claimed oneness with His Father.

"I and the Father are one."

John 10:30

2. He also claimed oneness with the Holy Spirit. Part of Jesus' last instructions were for His disciples to baptize in the name of the Father, and the Son and the Holy Spirit. From the RYRIE STUDY BIBLE (Moody Press), we read: "Here is evidence for the trinity of God: one God (the name) who subsists in three persons (Father, Son and Holy Spirit). Each of the three is distinguished from the others; each possesses all the divine attributes; yet the three are one. This is a mystery which no analogy can illustrate satisfactorily. The sun, sunlight, and the power of the sun may come close to a suitable illustration."

Now, how do these facts convince us we should do things as Jesus would? Why should we pattern our lives after Him? **Jesus Christ is the God of the Old Testament. He made the world. He's also the physical revelation of the invisible God and a co-equal with God the Father and God the Holy Spirit.** The only way we can come to know God the Father is through Jesus Christ (John 14:6). When we hear Jesus speak, we hear God speak. When we understand how and why Jesus did things, we understand God's ways.

Jesus made the most astonishing claim of all when He claimed equality with His Father. Yet, His life backed up His claim with profound teaching, amazing miracles climaxed by His resurrection from the dead! The rest of God's word confirms His equality with the Father. Prophecy proves it! **When we pattern our lives after Jesus Christ, we're patterning our lives after the holy and perfect God who made this entire universe and created us.** Jesus Christ is God! And, that makes Him the only One worthy enough to be followed with a total commitment from you and me!

FOR INDEPENDENT AND GROUP STUDY

1. Explain how prophecy concerning the Messiah backs up the claims Jesus made about Himself.

2. The Bible tells us that Jesus was the Word that became flesh (John 1:14). How does that truth relate to our being obedient to other portions of the Bible, as well as to the earthly life and teachings of Jesus Christ?

"IF POSSIBLE, SO FAR AS IT DEPENDS ON YOU, BE AT PEACE WITH ALL MEN."

Romans 12:18

CHAPTER THREE

THE FIRST STEP

Perhaps you've been intrigued with the idea of becoming Christ-like. Well, like anything else, this process must have a beginning. **And, the beginning of Christ-likeness is to first commit yourself to Jesus Christ, a commitment that Jesus, Himself, referred to as being "born again" (John 3:3).** It's a commitment where you give the leadership of your life over to Jesus Christ, and depend on Him for your eternal destiny as well as for each day. And, it's the first step we must all take before we can become Christ-like. Ironically, it can't be done on your own effort alone. God must first create within you the desire to make that commitment. This chapter is written with you in mind, if God has begun to draw you to Himself, but for one reason or another you've never made that commitment. We'll approach how to take that first step by answering some of the most frequently asked questions about taking it, as well as what happens after it's taken.

1. I know the Bible talks a lot about sin. But what does sin really mean?

The word "sin" is an archery term. It means "missing the mark." The "sin-mark" is that distance between the bulls-eye on a target and the actual place where your arrow hits. It measures the distance between perfection and where you're really at in accuracy.

When the Bible tells us we've sinned, it's describing our missing the mark of God's perfection. We fall short of His standard in our attitudes, thoughts and actions. And that creates a problem! A holy and perfect God can't have fellowship with a sinful and imperfect man. There's no possible way, on our own power, to have close fellowship with God in our sin condition. We don't have anything in common with Him. And that's what fellowship is all about. Having things

Sin means missing the mark.

in common with others. Just as oil can't mix with water, neither can sin mix with God.

"For the wages [penalty] of sin is **death** [eternal separation from God]..."

Romans 6:23

The result of our sinful state is an eternal separation from God. Unless something is done, we can never personally know God and have close fellowship with Him.

2. Well, I might miss the mark of God's perfection, but I'm not so bad when I look at other people. Doesn't God take that into consideration?

Even people who compare favorably with others still fall short of God's perfection. Let's say a few people want to jump over a canyon. The first person runs to the edge and takes off with a mighty leap. He sails out about 23 feet and then crashes to the canyon bottom. The next person really puts some extra effort into it. He doesn't want to end up like the first, so he has an even better takeoff. In fact, he sails out over 27 feet! He feels good that he outjumped the first person, but he also fell short of the other side. Both end up at the bottom of the canyon! Another person with rockets attached to his back also falls short. Now, who really is better off? They all ended up at the bottom of the canyon!

The same thing is true of our personal lives. It doesn't matter how well we compare with other people. On our own merits, we still fall short of God's perfection and can't have close fellowship with Him in that condition.

"...for **all** have sinned and **fall short** of the glory of God..."

Romans 3:23

No one is exempt. Everyone is guilty of sinning against God.

3. Then how can anyone become part of God's family if it's not a matter of being morally better than others?

That's where Jesus Christ comes in. Let's take a quick overview of His life right now. As we do, I think you'll get a good idea of how Jesus Christ has made it possible for us to come into God's family.

Jesus came from Nazareth, a poorly thought of village in Galilee. He was a carpenter by trade, and knew what hard work, slivers in His hands and sweat were all about. From first-hand experience, He knew about poverty and what it was to have people prejudiced against Him. At about 30 years of age Jesus began His public teaching. When He talked, though He didn't have a formal education, people said He spoke with amazing authority. He gave sight to the blind, healed lepers, walked on water and raised the dead. Yet, those who knew Him best, claimed His greatest work was changing them into new people!

Jesus made many thought-provoking statements about Himself. He said, "I am the way, and the truth, and the life; no one comes to the Father, but through Me" (John 14:6), "I and the Father are one" (John 10:30), and "I came that they might have life, and might have it abundantly" (John 10:10).

But, there were those who didn't agree with Him, mainly the religious leaders. They said no man was God, and because Jesus claimed to be God they accused him of blasphemy. They trumped up charges against Him, spit on Him, ripped the skin off His back with a whip, beat His face beyond recognition and then nailed Him to a cross. At noon, total darkness came over the land and lasted for three hours. At the end of that time, He was separated from His Father in payment for our rebellion against God. And, He died! His enemies thought they were finally rid of Him, but on the third day He rose from the dead. Later, He appeared to friends on many different occasions and to over 500 people at one time. Before onlookers eyes He ascended into heaven. And, equally amazing, He said He would return!

So, how did Jesus make it possible for you and me to come into God's family? **He took care of the penalty for our sins.** You see, it's our sins, and the penalty payment we owe for them, that keeps us from having close fellowship with God in His family. When Jesus paid the penalty for us by His suffering and death on the cross, God forgave us all of our sins in much the same way we'd be forgiven a financial debt if someone paid it for us. But our penalty could only be paid by someone who wasn't guilty of sin, someone who was perfect. Jesus Christ!

> "He [God] made Him [Jesus Christ] who knew no sin to be sin **on our behalf** [take our place on the cross], that we might become the righteousness of God in Him [God sees the perfection of Jesus Christ in us]."
>
> 2 Corinthians 5:21

It's incredible what Jesus did for us, isn't it? We can't imagine how He must have suffered to pay the penalty for our sins. He didn't owe any penalty, Himself, because He never sinned. But out of His love for us, He paid our penalty! Jesus made it possible for us to stand before God as totally forgiven.

4. It sounds as though Jesus did it all for me. Isn't there anything I have to do?

Yes, in order for His payment of your penalty to be personally valid, you have to accept what Jesus Christ did for you as well as believe in Him.

> "But as many as **received** Him, to them He gave the right to become children of God, even to those who **believe** in His name..."
>
> John 1:12

"Receiving Him" means you personally accept Him and all He said and did. That includes His payment of your penalty! Just as a governor's pardon isn't legally valid until it's accepted by the prisoner, neither is what Jesus Christ did for you personally valid until you accept it for yourself.

The words "believe in His name" doesn't refer to simply knowing some facts about Jesus. They refer to a reliance on

Him that begins right here in this lifetime and continues throughout eternity with Him. "Believe" is a word used to describe what a person does when he accepts something as true and relies upon it as a way of life. It's more than an intellectual agreement. **It's betting your life on it!** I think this popular illustration might help us appreciate what "believe" really means.

One day a tightrope walker walked above a roaring waterfall. Hundreds of people gathered to watch his every step. They were amazed as he walked across. Then he took a wheelbarrow across flawlessly. Again he received a tremendous ovation. He asked the audience if they believed he could safely wheel a man across the waterfall. "Sure we do!" they exclaimed. Then he motioned for an enthusiastic man down front to get into the wheelbarrow. That man was still enthusiastic, but this time he was enthusiastically refusing to get into the wheelbarrow.

You see, this man had an intellectual belief in the tightrope walker. He believed the man could do some amazing things on the highwire. But, there was no way he was going to put his life in the hands of that man. **When you have the John 1:12 kind of belief in Jesus, you're relying on Him with your life.** You're saying you're putting your life in His hands and want Him to be the center of everything you do. That's a big first step. It's more than just knowing some things about Jesus. It's committing yourself to enthusiastically follow Him as a new way of life. Perhaps the following Self Evaluation will help you more clearly understand what this first step toward Christ-likeness involves.

SELF EVALUATION

Your belief in Jesus Christ means you accept and rely on these basic truths:

A. Jesus Christ is God (John 8:24 and 10:30). Do you believe that?

☐ Yes   ☐ No

B. Jesus Christ took your place on the cross. Through His death He paid the penalty for your sins (2 Corinthians 5:21). Do you believe this and personally accept His payment on your behalf?

☐ Yes   ☐ No

C. Jesus Christ was buried and then was raised from the dead (Matthew 28:6 and 1 Corinthians 15:4). Do you believe that?

☐ Yes   ☐ No

Also, your belief in Jesus Christ acknowledges that:

A. You no longer want to live for yourself, but want Jesus Christ to take control of your life and lead you in God's way of doing things (Galatians 2:20 and Philippians 1:21). Is that what you desire?

☐ Yes   ☐ No

B. You want His attitudes, thoughts and actions to be yours (2 Corinthians 10:5). Do you want that?

☐ Yes   ☐ No

If your answer has been "yes" to all of these questions, you're a Christian and in God's eternal family. And, you've taken the first step in becoming Christ-like.

5. I believe in Jesus Christ that way. But, is there any tangible way I can express my belief in Him?

Yes, you can talk to God about your belief in Jesus Christ. Often, talking to God can help cement what we believe in our own minds. If you desire, you can use the following prayer. But, the words of this prayer are important only in that they represent what's in your heart. So, if they do represent what you believe, you can make them your own right now.

> "Dear God. Thank you for sending Your Son, Jesus Christ, to pay the penalty for my sin, and for revealing yourself to me through Him. I accept what you've done for me and accept your Son into my life. I commit myself to His leadership. Amen!"

Remember, the words of this prayer didn't make you a Christian. Your **belief** in Jesus Christ did!

6. I feel close to God right now. But what if I don't in a few days? Does that mean I'm not in His family anymore?

No. Your emotion now, or in a few days, has nothing to do with you being in God's family. In fact, it's quite possible you don't have any special feelings right now. **God hasn't accepted you into His family on the basis of your emotion, but on the basis of your belief in Jesus Christ.** And, your relationship with God, based upon that belief, **can never be broken!** You'll always be in God's family throughout all eternity! Jesus said, "My sheep hear My voice, and I know them, and they follow Me; and I give eternal life to them, and they shall never perish; and no one shall snatch them out of My hand" (John 10:27-28). Just as you'll always be a member of your earthly family in this lifetime, regardless of your feelings, so you'll always be a member of God's family because of what Jesus did for you and your acceptance of it, regardless of how you feel.

7. Is there anything you can suggest to help me grow stronger in my reliance on Jesus Christ now that I've taken this first step?

Although this book will help you become better acquainted

with Him, and show you some steps to take in becoming more Christ-like, **there's no substitute for the Bible.** The Bible is God's word to you personally. And, as you read His words in the Bible, He, Himself, will help you understand how to apply His truths to your life. If you don't already own a Bible, you might consider buying a modern translation at a local Christian bookstore. Some good ones to consider are The New American Standard Bible, The New International Version, Good News for Modern Man, and The New Testament in Modern English by J.B.Phillips.

The best place to start reading the Bible is in the Gospels of Mark or John where you'll become better acquainted with the One you've committed yourself to follow. **I've found I get more out of what I read in the Bible if I'm looking for answers to questions I have.** For instance, as you're reading either Mark or John, you might be asking, "What does this verse tell me about God?" Or, "What qualities in Jesus Christ's life do I notice are lacking in mine?" You'll see finding answers to specific questions helps you retain and apply more of what you read. Also, visit your local Christian bookstore for books that will help you read, memorize and study God's word. Then, you're on your way!

Now, that you've taken this important first step of committing yourself to follow Jesus Christ, you're ready to plunge in and see what else is involved in becoming Christ-like. **You've taken the first step and you have ahead of you the greatest adventure anyone could ever experience!**

FOR INDEPENDENT AND GROUP STUDY

1. Why can't a holy God have fellowship with a sinful man apart from the work of Jesus Christ on the cross?

2. Why can't you be accepted into God's family on the basis of your good works?

3. Why can't you simply believe there is a God and be in His family?

4. What does the word "believe" in John 1:12 really mean?

5. On the basis of Philippians 1:9-11, what is God's desire for you as a Christian?

"THEREFORE IF ANY MAN IS IN CHRIST, HE IS A NEW CREATURE; THE OLD THINGS PASSED AWAY; BEHOLD, NEW THINGS HAVE COME."

2 Corinthians 5:17

CHAPTER FOUR

NOW, THAT'S WHAT I CALL A GOAL!

Diane was hurriedly doing the dinner dishes as she noticed her husband sitting in his favorite chair reading some papers from his briefcase. "Jim honey, could you help me with these dishes?" she anxiously asked. "I'm already late for my meeting!"

"I can't believe it!" Jim replied. It was obvious he was irritated with Diane's request. "Diane, you know how important it is for me to work on this report! It can mean a promotion for us!" Diane was disappointed in her husband's response to her request. "Jim," she exploded, "you know that promotion isn't important to the kids and me. It's only important to you. We don't need what that promotion will buy. We just need more of you!"

"You're a great one to talk," replied Jim angrily. "This just happens to be how I make a living! And I can't sit back and let promotions slip by just because you don't think we need one!" Diane, softening a little, said, "Oh, Jim, all you ever do is work, even when you don't have to. I'm not sure the kids even know you!" Exasperated, Jim came back, "Well what's so important about the meeting you're going to tonight? And the one you went to two nights ago? You wouldn't have time for me even if I did give it to you. You're too busy doing your own things!"

And so it goes. Jim and Diane sound familiar, don't they? **Jim's goal was to get to the top of his world and build his own little Fort Knox. Diane was wrapped up in the home, kids and meetings.** Deep down they really did want togetherness but they just couldn't let go of going after their own interests. Yet, they're not different than most of us, are they?

We all want different things. The wife might want a new dishwasher and the husband might want a set of golf clubs. Which one does the money buy? We aim towards so many conflicting things it's hard to have harmony. A report or meeting, versus time with the family. A set of golf clubs versus a new dishwasher. Is this how God intended the Christian life to be lived? Everyone pursuing his own interests? I can confidently say, on the authority of God's word, it isn't! I **believe our greatest problem today is that we each seek various goals we've set for ourselves without considering God's goal for us.** Let's quickly explore five passages from the Bible to get a better picture of what **God's one goal** for us is. You'll notice one central theme weaving it's way through each of these passages.

> 1. "For whom He foreknew, He also predestined to **become conformed to the image of His Son** that He might be the first born among many brethren."
>
> Romans 8:29

"Conformed" refers to an inner transformation of our attitudes and thoughts to those of Jesus which results in our actions reflecting those He would have. **God desires us to be-**

come just like Jesus Christ. This is a continuous process of development that will one day reach its fulfillment when we're in His actual presence (1 John 3:2-3).

> 2. "...the one who says he abides in Him ought himself to **walk in the same manner as He [Jesus] walked.**"
>
> 1 John 2:6

"Walk" is a word John used to describe a way of living. For us to walk in the same manner as Jesus walked would be to live the same way He lived. We'd hear things through His "ears," see things through His "eyes" and understand things with His "heart." **Our values would be His and our actions would reflect them.**

> 3. "For you have been called for this purpose, for Christ also suffered for you, **leaving you an example for you to follow in His steps...**"
>
> 1 Peter 2:21

Again, "follow in His steps" conveys a way of living. The idea here is we're to see Christ's sacrificial way of life as an example for us to give up our personal rights for the benefit of others. **He's our example as well as our leader.**

> 4. "Therefore, **we are ambassadors for Christ** as though God were entreating through us..."
>
> 2 Corinthians 5:20

Jesus came to direct man's attention to God the Father. Everything He did was calculated to focus our attention on our Creator. And, He's handed that mission over to us as His disciples. **God wants to speak to the world through our lives just as He did through Jesus.** In essence, we're ambassadors for Christ to carry out the mission He had while physically on earth. That means we have the responsibility of knowing what He'd do and doing it throughout the day.

> 5. "My children, with whom I am again in labor until **Christ is formed in you...**"
>
> Galatians 4:19

It's interesting the word "formed" is written in the passive voice. **This means it's God's responsibility, in the person of the Holy Spirit, to form Christ in us.** He could do this overnight if He desired, but He has chosen to do it through our following His ways.

These and over 120 passages in the New Testament teach us **God's main desire and goal for us is that we become Christ-like in everything we do.** Let's get down to the basics. If this is God's main goal for us, doesn't it stand to reason that our lives won't be totally fulfilled unless it becomes our main goal as well? What would be different in your life if you were determined to be Christ-like throughout each day?

Let's catch a glimpse of how things could have been different for Jim and Diane. If Diane was really pondering what Jesus would do in her situation of doing the dishes, she might have seen things differently. First, she might have realized the dishes really didn't have to be done before she left for the meeting. It was her desire to get them done, but it wasn't a necessity. As Jesus dined with Mary and Martha one day (Luke 10:38-42), it was Martha's desire to put on all of the trimmings. But those trimmings weren't necessary in order to have the type of fellowship Jesus wanted. It was just Martha's personal desire to have everything "just right." In the same way, doing the dishes was Diane's personal desire to leave things "in proper order." But, quite possibly it wasn't something that should have had priority at that particular moment.

Had Diane pondered what Jesus would do, she also might have seen that Jim was heavily engrossed in what he was doing. What he was doing might not have been God's highest priority for him at that time, but he was already into it. She could have shown Jim she had respect for him if she first would have asked if he could leave what he was doing to help her. Jesus showed individual respect to people throughout His ministry. For instance, one day as He came into a town and the villagers were pressing close to get a look at Him, He noticed Zacchaeus, a tax collector of poor reputation, in a tree gazing down at Him (Luke 19:1-10). Jesus stopped and told Zacchaeus He wanted to spend the night with him and his family. Zacchaeus became a new man after that visit. And, it all began when Jesus showed respect for him as a person even though He didn't always respect how Zacchaeus did things. Diane might not have respected what Jim was doing, but she could have communicated her respect to him, as a person, by being more considerate of him.

Also, had Diane been pondering what Jesus would do, she might have evaluated whether or not the meeting she was supposed to attend really was God's highest priority for her. Again, as we go back to the dinner scene of Jesus, Mary and Martha, we can see what Martha personally desired wasn't really necessary from God's perspective.

Now, let's take a look at how Jim might have handled the situation differently if he had been pondering what Jesus would do. First, just as Jesus was sensitive to His disciples' needs, Jim could have been more sensitive to Diane's needs. Rightly or wrongly she did have a need! She didn't need a lecture on whether the meeting was proper or not. She was pressed for time and had to leave. We see this kind of sensitivity from Jesus even when His attention could rightfully have been focused on His own needs. One occasion was in the upper room, following what has been termed The Last Supper (John 13:1-20). He knew He was about to be betrayed and killed. But in those turbulent moments, when all of His attention could have been turned inwardly, He got on His knees and washed His disciples' feet. Why? To communicate His sincere love for them. Had Jim been representing Jesus at that moment, possibly he could have given Diane the helping hand she needed. And, he might even have done the whole job for her to give her a couple of extra minutes before she had to leave. Why? To communicate his love for her!

Also, had Jim pondered what Jesus would do, and been committed to do it, he might not have been working on his report at that particular time of evening. We see, from Jesus' life, He was always in the right place at the right time. He wasn't lagging behind in Capernaum, although He was greatly popular there, when He should have been on His way to Jerusalem to be crucified. He was sensitive to what was important at each moment. Sure, it was important to heal people back in Capernaum. But there came a time when the importance of going to the cross and doing the best thing outweighed the importance of remaining in Capernaum and doing a good thing. Representing Jesus doesn't mean Jim shouldn't have kept on working for his promotion. Just not at the expense of time with his family! He wouldn't be able to build the strong home God desired for him without spending quality time with his wife and children. Instead of working on his report at that moment, Jim might have been communicating with Diane or reading his children a bedtime story.

Another thing Jim might have done differently, if he had pondered how Jesus would have done it, would have been to speak gently to Diane in her moment of need. Even if he would have concluded Jesus wanted him to continue working on the report, Jim could have gently communicated his unavailability rather than have spoken so harshly to Diane.

Life definitely would have been different in Jim and Diane's household that evening had they both pondered what Jesus would do in their situations and committed themselves to do it. Of course, knowing exactly what Jesus would do in every situation takes time. It doesn't happen overnight. Had they known what He would have done, and been committed to do it, the Holy Spirit would have given them His power to do it. And, as a result each one of them would have been conformed more to the likeness of Jesus Christ. Even if only one of them had been representing Jesus that evening, things would have been different.

After talking to many Christians who indicate a desire to become more Christ-like, I've found very few are actually aiming at Christ-likeness. It's a desire with no apparent plan for accomplishment. The men of our local church meet together every Tuesday morning for fellowship in God's word. After we wade through the sports scores and hunting stories, we discuss how to apply biblical principles to everyday living. One morning one of these men suggested we quit putting all of our energies into reaching our natural goals and put them into becoming Christ-like in what we're doing. He wasn't saying we should quit our jobs, or drop out of what we're doing, but that we should put as much energy into becoming Christ-like as we put into our other endeavors. Most of these men did desire to become Christ-like, but had no plan of action.

Another example of Christians desiring to become Christ-like, but with no apparent plan to accomplish it, was a group of Christian college students. They came to our training center in Prescott to study how they could more perfectly live their lives according to God's word. These students had already attended two seminars we had conducted at their college. So, they knew the answer to the question I asked, "What's your goal?"

"To become conformed to the image of Jesus Christ," they all responded. "That's good," I replied. "But do you really mean it?" They all enthusiastically nodded yes. "How many of you can tell me 90% of everything Jesus said or did?"

Their enthusiasm turned to stunned silence. They weren't ready for that question. "Well then, how many of you can tell me 50% of everything Jesus said or did?" Still no hands. When I finally brought it down to 5%, one student timidly raised his hand. They all got the point. **If being conformed to the likeness of Christ really was their main goal, they'd have had a plan to help make it a reality.**

If you have a goal, you do things to achieve it, don't you? For instance, if going on a vacation is a goal, you begin to make plans. You see, we work at achieving our natural goals. We know what we need to do to earn a degree. We know how much we have to save to get the dishwasher or golf clubs. We know what we have to do to get a promotion. We work at getting things we really want. Now, don't get me wrong. I'm **not** advocating a "do it yourself" plan toward Christ-likeness. That's not how God designed the Christian life to be lived. Yet, He has given us the responsibility of willfully doing those things that Jesus would do. Then, through the Holy Spirit, He enables us to carry out those actions. The eye opener for the men at our breakfast, and for those Christian college students, was **we really do have a responsibility in becoming Christ-like.** And, they found out they hadn't taken any steps to pursue the one goal God had for them, to become Christ-like in everything they do.

SELF EVALUATION

1. Do you desire to become Christ-like in everything you do?

☐ Yes ☐ No

2. To become Christ-like, we need to get to know Jesus better than we do our best friend. Then, it'll be easier to understand what He'd do in all of our various situations. Also, because Jesus is the Word of God (John 1:14), and He taught from all of the Scriptures, we need to explore all parts of God's word to learn how He wants us to live our lives. Have you taken steps, outside of attending a church service, to become better acquainted with Jesus and learn what He wants you to do in various situations?

☐ Yes ☐ No

> **3. Do you know what Jesus would do in the various situations you face throughout the day?**
>
> ☐ Most of the time   ☐ Sometimes
>
> ☐ Hardly ever

Now, is it really possible to know what Jesus would do in our shoes throughout the day? After all, He never dated. He never studied for a final exam or decided which TV program to watch. He never negotiated a contract or had to run a household. He never had to choose between buying a dishwasher or a set of golf clubs. Jesus just didn't face a lot of things we do today. So, how do we know what He'd do in our situations?

Maybe this illustration will help communicate how we can know what He'd do even though He hasn't faced our same situations. I remember the first time I saw my wife, Peggy. She was walking a few feet away from me after watching a wrestling match at UCLA's Pauley Pavilion. A friend told me her name and where she worked, and meeting her became a top priority for me. Dating began and romance developed. A year later we were married!

Now, the day we were married I could honestly say we knew each other very well. But over eight years have passed and we know each other far better now than we did that first day of marriage. In fact, we know each other so well now that you could ask me what Peggy would do or say in various situations she might never have faced, and I could most likely tell you what her response would be. How's that possible? Because the more intimately I know Peggy, the easier it is to know how she'd think or act in various situations.

It's the same with knowing what Jesus would do in situations He never faced in His earthly life. **The more intimately I know Him, the easier it is to know what He'd do.** For instance, although He never looked at television, I know He'd only want me to watch programs that are edifying. He wouldn't want me to put a lot of wrong values in my mind (Philippians 4:8). Because of that I've become more selective in which programs I watch. Although He never drove a car down a freeway, I know He'd want me to abide by the legal speed limit since God's word teaches me to abide by governing authorities (Romans 13:1). And, although Jesus never had a wife, I know He'd want me to spend quality time with mine to develop strong family bonds. God's word teaches me to love my wife as Christ loved the church (Ephesians 5:25). You see, the more intimately I know Jesus, and all of God's word, the easier it is to know what He'd do in my situations.

So, getting to know Him intimately has to be part of our plan if we're ever to become more Christ-like. Studying the 15 episodes of Christ's life, analyzed in this book, should only be a beginning. The Bible is filled with episodes in Christ's life as well as with instructions for Christ-like living. We need to pursue Christ-likeness with at least the same enthusiasm we'd have in pursuing a promotion, vacation, or getting a new dishwasher or set of golf clubs.

> "But seek first His kingdom and His righteousness [which includes Jesus and His way]; and all these things shall be added to you."
>
> Matthew 6:33

Most of us have been busy seeking "these things" first, haven't we? Yet, God has designed us to be fulfilled only by seeking Him first. That's His goal for us. That's why it has to become our main goal!

"Where's the balance?" I can hear you ask. "After all, I still have to live in a pretty materialistically-oriented world. For example, what's wrong with aiming at a certain financial level?" There's nothing wrong with attaining a certain financial level. The wrongness comes in pursuing it as your main goal instead of letting it be the by-product of running your business the way Jesus would. And, there's nothing wrong with achieving a college degree, working on a report to get a promotion, going to a meeting, buying a dishwasher or buying a set of golf clubs. **The wrongness comes only if those things aren't what Jesus would be doing in your situations.** For example, would Jesus cheat to get the college degree? Of course not! In the Bible we learn that Jesus was above reproach. He didn't do anything that would cause people to think He was immoral in what He did. Would He sacrifice His family for the sake of obtaining a promotion? Negative again! God's word gives us many instructions on how to develop a close family life. Financial levels, promotions, reports, meetings, material possessions can all be considered natural goals. God's plan might involve us in many of these areas. But, unless we're careful to handle them His way, they can easily be classified under the category of "these things" in Matthew 6:33. **Our first responsibility is to pursue Christ-likeness in whatever area we're involved.** God will then bring us the financial levels, promotions, etc. if it pleases Him and He wants us to have them.

Working toward Christ-likeness, as the Holy Spirit empowers you, isn't easy to do in a world where we've been taught to pursue our natural desires. For instance, not long ago a good friend returned from elk hunting with a bow. He brought home 300 pounds of quartered elk meat. As my wife and I stood watching him wheel the meat into a locker, my wife commented, "Isn't it amazing that an arrow could bring down such a large animal?" My friend replied rather lowly, "Don't let this get around, but one of my hunting partner's brought it down with a bullet and he gave it to me." He went on to explain that the elk was a female and he was the only one in the hunting party with a tag to hunt a cow elk. He said he tagged it because he didn't want his friend to get in trouble for shooting it illegally. And, he saw it as an opportunity to put meat in his freezer!

The next day I asked my friend how he could justify accepting meat that was illegally taken. It was archery season and no elk should have been shot with a rifle. Now, the main reason I confronted him was because he's a Christian committed to do things as Jesus would. And, according to Luke 17:3, I've got a responsibility to rebuke my Christian brother if he's sinning (missing the mark). The more he tried to rationalize his actions, the more he became convinced he'd done the wrong thing. He was especially convinced when he read that God wants us to obey civil authorities (Romans 13:1-2).

He thought about it for quite awhile and then decided to give up the meat. What a tough decision it was! He was financially broke and really could have used that food. In market value he was giving up more than $500 worth of meat! Naturally, some people thought he was foolish. But, from his perspective, he had to be true to his convictions and his commitment to become Christ-like in everything he did. It was a struggle for him, but his desire to be Christ-like won out.

Our struggles in becoming more Christ-like will involve raising our children and loving our mate. They'll involve deciding which meetings to attend and classes to take as well as what to do in leisure activities. They'll involve budgeting our income as well as being selective in which television programs to watch. **But, the end result of these struggles is Christ-likeness. And that's worth it!** Not only will the Holy Spirit help us do things God's way while here on earth, but God will **reward** us for doing them His way after this life is over.

> "Therefore, whether we are at home [on earth away from Him], or away from home [and with Him], **we are constantly ambitious and strive earnestly to be well-pleasing to Him.** For we must all appear and be revealed as we are before the judgment seat of Christ, so that **each one may receive [his pay] according to what he has done in the body,** whether good or evil, [considering what his purpose and motive have been, and what he has achieved, been busy with and given himself and his attention to accomplishing].
>
> 2 Corinthians 5:9-10, The Amplified Bible

Becoming Christ-like in everything he did was the greatest ambition of the apostle Paul. He constantly worked at being well-pleasing to Christ. That was God's desire for him just as it is for you and me. And, Paul knew that one day he would stand before Jesus Christ and receive eternal rewards for those things he did God's way. The same is true for us. **We'll also stand before Jesus Christ and be rewarded for those things we did with Christ-like attitudes, thoughts and actions.** A large portion of this book has been designed to help you have biblical handles to make Christ-likeness a daily reality.

FOR INDEPENDENT AND GROUP STUDY

1. What was the root problem Jim and Diane had? Does their situation in any way relate to your own life at home or at work? Please explain.

2. What is God's goal for the believer?

3. Explain how each of the five Bible passages, given in this chapter, relates to God's goal for us?

4. List some attitudes or actions in your life in which you frequently have difficulty being Christ-like. Explain how two or three of them would be different if you consciously pursued Christ-likeness in those areas.

5. What is your responsibility in becoming Christ-like?

6. What is God's responsibility in bringing us into more Christ-likeness?

7. Since Jesus didn't face many of the same situations we do today, how can we actually know what He would do in our situations?

8. Since Jesus Christ is our ultimate example for Christ-likeness, what role does the rest of God's word have in our becoming Christ-like?

9. Is there one particular goal you have been pursuing that can actually conflict with, or hinder, God's one goal for you to become Christ-like in everything you do? If so, please explain.

CHAPTER FIVE

HEY, CHEER UP YOU'RE REALLY LOVED!

What are some of the **greatest ways** you can think of for expressing your love to a friend? Think about it for a moment. Maybe it's writing a letter to your friend when you're rushed and have many other things to do. It could be giving a large amount of money you've been saving for a house to meet a friend's medical expenses. Or, perhaps it's to give of your time by visiting him 30 afternoons in a row while he's hospitalized. It might be giving up your right to have privacy by having a needy friend live with you and eat your food when you're short of space and are financially strapped. Maybe the greatest thing you can do for a friend is to help fix his car.

There's no doubt that any of these things would certainly communicate your love. And, most of us would consider them great. But, as great as they are, they can't compare to the answer Jesus gave. **He said, "Greater love has no one than this, that one lay down his life for his friends" (John 15:13).** This is carrying things to an extreme, isn't it? We would find that a very difficult thing to do even for the best of friends. Well, it wasn't easy for Jesus either. But that's exactly how far He went to communicate His love for you and me.

I'm convinced that one of the greatest reasons we don't have an all-out commitment to live for God by doing things His way is because **we take Him and His love for granted.** We forget the horrifying experience Jesus must have endured during His crucifixion as well as the events leading up to it. He endured not only the excruciating pain of the scourge and the cross, but also the spiritual and emotional pain of being separated from His Father while paying for our sins. We can't begin to imagine the full impact of what He experienced. But, in this chapter we'll make an attempt to better understand what Jesus went through physically, spiritually, emotionally and mentally to communicate how much He really loves us. **It's my hope that we never again take His love for granted!**

Let's capture the flavor of that event that took place almost 2000 years ago. It was approximately 11 o'clock at night when Jesus and His men made their way through a ravine called the Valley of Kidron. The moon was full, as it always was that time of year, at the Jewish Passover celebration. And, on that moonlit night, Jesus might have noticed blood from the temple sacrifices mixing with the water from the Brook of Kidron as He crossed over the brook on His way to the Garden of Gethsemane. Blood drained into the brook from the temple above where they slaughtered animals preparing for the Passover. **What a grim reminder it would have been that Jesus, too, would be sacrificed!**

When Jesus and His men reached the Garden of Gethsemane, He left eight of His companions at the entrance and took three with Him into the inner part of the garden. After asking the three to keep awake, and to watch with Him and pray, He went a little further into the garden and literally cast Himself on the ground. Three times He prayed in great agony, "Father, remove this cup from Me." The word "cup" means the portion of life He was facing. He was saying, "Father, I don't want to go through with this! Can't we do it some other way?" Yet, each time He concluded His request by saying it wasn't what He wanted that counted, but what His Father wanted. **And, He was committed to doing His Father's will.**

We can't begin to visualize His torment. While His men slept, Jesus was in such great inner turmoil that the perspiration pouring off His body was similar to how great drops of blood would gush out of a wound. All this in the cool of the evening! After much agonizing prayer, He looked across the valley and saw a mob of soldiers and religious leaders coming His way with swords, spears and clubs. Most authorities believe this mob numbered up to 600. These soldiers were expertly trained to either kill or take captive, and Jesus knew they were coming for Him. **What would you have done if you were in Jesus' sandals and saw that mob coming after you?** I would have run so fast that my sandals would still have been in the garden!

But Jesus calmly awakened His men for the third time and told them the time had come. Then, He led them to the garden entrance where the mob had already approached His other disciples. You can imagine how shook all of the disciples must have been to see approximately 600 soldiers and religious leaders surrounding them.

After Judas pointed Jesus out to the soldiers with the customary kiss of welcome, Jesus walked up to the soldiers and asked, "Who do you want?" They said, "Jesus of Nazareth. Where is He?" When Jesus answered, "I am He," they fell backwards on the ground.

Can you picture a mob of approximately 600 people falling backwards on the ground? It wasn't because Jesus was such an awesome figure physically. These soldiers wouldn't have blinked an eye if 100 of the world's strongest men were standing there. They were well-trained and disciplined fighting men. We really can't know for sure why they fell to the ground as the Bible doesn't give us an explanation. Possibly, at that moment, they caught a glimpse of God's grandeur in Jesus and fell over in awe.

Jesus went up to them again and asked, "Who do you want?" Again they replied, "Jesus!" This time when He said, "I am He," they seized Him. Just then Peter went into action. Can you believe it? With several hundred armed soldiers surrounding them, Peter drew a sword to defend Jesus. We probably can't say a lot about the practical side of Peter at that point, but we can say he sure was brave and loyal. Peter raised his sword and swiftly brought it down. Instead of hitting the middle of his victim's head, as was the strategy of using that particular sword, he sliced an ear off one of the men. Can you see it? Here's a man looking at his ear on the ground, and there stands Peter with a sword in his hand surrounded by several hundred Roman soldiers. I can imagine Peter looking at Jesus as if to say, "We're in a heap of trouble now, Master!"

Jesus told Peter to put away his sword because those who live by the sword die by it. And, Peter probably didn't waste anytime putting it up. Then Jesus told Peter, "Don't you realize I could bring in twelve legions of angels to save me?" That's 72,000 angels! Jesus would definitely have had the odds in His favor! But, Jesus didn't choose to do that, saying, "But how then should the scripture be fulfilled that it must come about this way?" **He had come from heaven for the very task ahead of Him -- His crucifixion!**

Jesus picked up the ear laying on the ground and placed it back on the man's head. You can imagine how surprised everyone was when the ear stayed in place when Jesus took His hand away. No glue. No stitches. Nothing but the power of God! Then Jesus gave Himself over to the mob and all but two of His disciples ran off. It's because of these two, Peter and John, following at a distance that we have an accurate account of what happened from that point on.

Why did Jesus give Himself up to the soldiers knowing the terrible ordeal ahead of Him? **It all had to do with how much He loves us!** He was committed to carrying out His Father's plan which would make it possible for you and me to come into God's family as forgiven people.

Jesus went through a series of six grossly unfair trials. All of them were illegal. We'll just briefly look at what went on at the first two before we capture a glimpse of His last trial before Pilate, the Roman governor.

The first trial was conducted by Annas, the former high priest. The purpose here was to get a charge against Jesus.

"What have You been teaching the people?" Annas asked Jesus. "If I tell you what I've been teaching," Jesus replied, "You won't believe me. Ask the people I've been talking to and they'll tell you the truth." An officer of the guard smashed Jesus with the heel of his hand, thinking Jesus had spoken disrespectfully to the former high priest. Jesus looked at the officer and said, "If I've said something that's wrong, tell Me what I've said that's wrong. But if I haven't said anything wrong, why did you hit Me?" No reply was recorded from the officer. Could it have been that he was awed when he came face to face with Jesus Christ? Or, could it have been the authority with which Jesus spoke?

Annas failed in getting a legitimate charge against Jesus, so he sent Him to Caiaphas, the current high priest. When Caiaphas asked Him if He was the Messiah, the Son of the living God, Jesus replied, "I am." Caiaphas tore his own clothes in anger and exclaimed to the jury that Jesus spoke blasphemy. He demanded a verdict from the jury. "Kill Him! Crucify Him!" was the verdict. "No one dares claim to be God. No man is God!"

The Jewish method of execution was stoning. **But, the Jewish religious authorities wanted Jesus crucified, which was a Roman method of execution.** So they took Jesus to Pilate, the Roman governor, to seek a sentence of crucifixion. When Pilate didn't see any wrong in Jesus, the religious leaders used a tactic that forced Pilate to play into their hands. They said Jesus claimed to be a king, but Jewish people were only supposed to pay tribute to Caesar, the Roman emperor. They accused Jesus of trying to create a rebellion among the Jewish people. And, that's exactly what Pilate didn't need! He was already in Caesar's "doghouse" because of other uprisings against the Roman tyranny. His position would be in danger if he allowed another one. **Pilate was in a predicament.** He didn't want to kill Jesus, but to show the people he was in control, he commanded Him to be scourged. **Scourging was a brutality just one step short of death.**

So, Jesus was stripped to the waist and either tied to a stake in the bent over position, or tied face down on the ground with His legs and arms outstretched. The Bible doesn't tell which way they scourged Him, but in either way the results were the same.

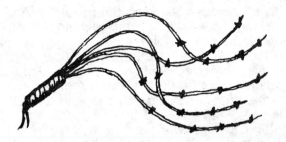

The scourge was a whip of three or more thongs, each having a sharp implement -- metal, bone or stone -- on the end that would easily dig into something as soft as flesh. One method of scourging was to hit the victim at the base of his neck. Then the scourge was violently pulled down the length of his back so the hooks tore the victim's flesh. One medical authority, who researched the effects of the scourge using dead bodies, said that between the 18th and 25th lash the skin would be completely stripped off a man's back. Between the 30th and 40th lash, if the man lasted that long, the flesh would be so badly torn apart you could push through it with your hands and see portions of the internal organs.

We don't know how many lashes Jesus received, but assuming Pilate wanted to convince the people of his desire to punish Jesus, it was probably as many as Jesus could take without dying. If Jesus had been tied to a stake, He would have been cut loose with His body slumping into a pool of His own blood. Why did He allow Himself to be scourged? Because of His love for you and me. **The greater the personal sacrifice, the greater the expression of love!**

Following the scourge, the soldiers pushed and slugged Jesus around. By the time He was taken to Pilate He had fulfilled the prophesy saying He would be beaten beyond recognition (Isaiah 52:14). When Pilate told the mob, "Look at Him," there wasn't much to look at anymore. Pilate wanted to let Him go, but the mob still cried for His blood. So, Pilate came to the decision at 6 o'clock Friday morning to crucify Him.

There were several ways to crucify someone, two were more common than others. One was to have the vertical beam already in the ground. The person would carry his own horizontal beam to the place where he was to be crucified. Then he would be staked onto the horizontal beam which would be lifted and set into a slot on the vertical beam. His feet would then be staked. Another way would be to stake the victim to the entire cross as it lay on the ground. The cross would then be lifted and dropped into the hole. Both methods had the same jarring effect on the victim.

Let's consider the second way as it would have applied to Jesus. Laying on the cross, Jesus' arms would have been stretched out as far as they could go. Then spikes would have been driven through His wrists between the carpal bones which are considered a part of the hand. The reason

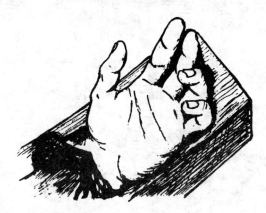

the Romans placed the spike between the carpal bones, and not in the palm of the hands, was to prevent the hands from ripping loose when the body's weight began pulling on them. Then they would have spiked Jesus' feet. Two or three Roman soldiers would then have lifted the cross dropping it into the hole. The cross would have stopped abruptly at the bottom of the hole, causing the staked body of Jesus to jerk downward on the cross. This jolt would have caused the extended ligaments in His shoulders to begin to tear. Before long, due to the weight of His sagging body, the shoulders would have become completely dislocated. The sagging body would have put pressure on His lungs and would have given Jesus the feeling of suffocation, similar to the feeling you get when the wind is knocked out of you. Jesus would have had to gasp for air. In order to stay alive He would have had to push up with His legs and hold Himself up for as long as He could while He caught a breath. Soon, the awkwardness of that upright position would have made Him drop again.

At 12 noon, total darkness lasting three hours came over the land. At 3 p.m. Jesus cried out, "My God, My God, why have you left Me? Why have you forsaken Me?" "Forsake" means to totally turn one's back on someone. **At that time, God the Father had to turn His back on His Son because Jesus took our sins on Himself. The One who hadn't sinned paid the penalty for all mankind's sins.** Jesus' last words on the cross were, "It is finished!" He meant, "I've paid your penalty. Go free and enjoy the life I've given you!"

I believe the following popular illustration can give us a small idea of the price God paid through His Son, Jesus, to communicate His love to us. There was a father who operated a drawbridge over a river. This father loved to be with his son and one day brought him to work with him. Everytime a boat drew near he'd lift the bridge and when a train approached he'd lower it. While the father was in the process of lowering the bridge for the 5 o'clock train, his son became entangled in the gears. As the train whistled it's approach, the father heard a scream from his son. To his horror the father saw his son being drawn into the giant jaws of the gears. The father had a split-second decision to make. If he raised the bridge to save his son, the train would plunge into the river killing hundreds of people. If he allowed his son to be crushed to death, the train would cross over the bridge and all of the people would be saved. In that split-second, the father made a decision that sent the one he loved most to an agonizing death.

It's ironic that, as the train passed over the bridge, not one person looked over at the little operator's stand and thanked

the father for what had happened. No one saw the tear-filled, anguished man slumped over his son. They never knew what the man gave up so they could be saved from death.

We can live our lives in much the same manner as those people passing by on the train, can't we? It's hard to imagine the agony Jesus experienced as He took on all of the filth and tragedy of mankind's sin. The pain of the scourge and crucifixion would have been bad enough. But that was just a fringe of the pain Jesus felt as He was totally separated from His Father in payment for our sins. **We can easily take His love for granted, can't we?**

If you've already personally accepted what Jesus has done for you, why not right now pause for a moment and thank Him again for what He's done? It might be a good time to acknowledge to Him that you sometimes take His love and sacrifice for granted. If you haven't yet accepted what Jesus Christ has done for you, why not right now consider accepting Him and thank Him for His great demonstration of love for you? (You can read Chapter Three for additional information on how to receive Jesus Christ into your life.)

Remember, you really are loved! Jesus didn't simply say, "I love you!" **He demonstrated His love for us by allowing Himself to suffer an agonizing and painful death. It was His expression of how much He really does love us!** The best way we can thank Him is by choosing to live for Him by lining up our attitudes, thoughts and actions with those of His. And, we can do that through His power in us!

FOR INDEPENDENT AND GROUP STUDY

1. Jesus said, "My food is to do the will of Him who sent Me, and to accomplish His work" (John 4:34). How does that desire on His part relate to His prayer in the Garden of Gethsemane?

2. Does knowing what Jesus went through on the cross for you have an impact on how you would like to do things in your home, work, etc. Please explain.

"LOOK AT THE BIRDS OF THE AIR, THAT THEY DO NOT SOW, NEITHER DO THEY REAP, NOR GATHER INTO BARNS, AND YET YOUR HEAVENLY FATHER FEEDS THEM. ARE YOU NOT WORTH MUCH MORE THAN THEY?"

Matthew 6:26

CHAPTER SIX

LOVE PRODUCES ACTION

Bob rushed excitedly into his house. Standing still momentarily, he heard voices of his two young children playing off in the distance. Finding his wife, Aleta, in the kitchen, he took her by the arm and said, "Come on, let's go into the other room. I've got something to tell you!"

"Bob, I can't right now," she replied. "I'm in the middle of preparing dinner!" But he couldn't hold it back. "We've got to sell our house and second car," he blurted out! Aleta, stunned, could only muster, "What?" "We've got to get rid of our luxuries!" Bob exclaimed. "But Bob, our house could hardly be called a luxury!"

"I had lunch with a guy today," he continued, "and he's really sold out for Jesus! He's living in a van just traveling around talking to people about Jesus!" "But Bob, we can't do that," interrupted Aleta, "we can't just sell everything we have and start traveling around like gypsies!"

Disappointed that his wife didn't share his enthusiasm, Bob replied, "Why not? Why do we have to keep living the same way just because we've always done it that way? Don't you understand what I'm talking about Aleta? I'm talking about a 100% commitment to Jesus Christ!"

"Bob," Aleta responded, "aren't you forgetting about the commitment Jesus wants you to fulfill to our two children and myself?" "No, of course not," Bob reasoned. "We'd all be together!" "But what about our financial responsibilities?" asked Aleta. "Even if we sold everything we owned, we'd still owe money." "Yeah, I know," replied Bob dejectedly, "I've got so many things tying me down! With all these responsibilities, how can I really be sold out to Jesus and live 100% for Him?"

SELF EVALUATION

1. If Jesus asked you to sell all of your material possessions, would you immediately do it without question?

☐ Yes   ☐ No

2. If following Jesus Christ meant you'd have to give up your family, would you do it?

☐ Yes   ☐ No

You don't want to answer these questions, do you? Maybe you even resent them. Well, relax. To my knowledge, He hasn't asked you or me to do either one. But would you, if He did? It's a sobering thought, isn't it?

Let's get the right perspective on what it means to be 100% committed to Jesus Christ. I think it's obvious Bob didn't have the right idea. To be 100% committed to Jesus Christ doesn't mean you can't have money or the material things it'll buy. It doesn't mean you can't have strong family bonds! **It's not what we have, but what has us.** It's what controls us! Questions like those in our Self Evaluation help point out our commitment to Him.

Jesus often used extremes to get His message across. For example, He said that unless we hated our father and mother, we couldn't be His disciples (Luke 14:26). Can you believe that? Sounds contradictory to other teachings of His, doesn't it? But let's look closer and see what He meant by "hate." He used the word to **compare** love for our parents to our love for Him. He meant unless our love for Him is far greater than our love for our father and mother, we can't be His true disciples. He wasn't telling us to hate our parents, only to love Him more than we love them, or anyone else.

Jesus once told a rich man, who asked Him how he might enter the kingdom of God, to sell all he had and give it to the poor. Now, Jesus wasn't against this man's wealth anymore than He'd be against your wealth. But, He saw this man was more committed to his wealth than to God. Unless he got his priorities straight, his wealth would keep him from entering the kingdom of God.

Even though Jesus hasn't asked you to get rid of your material possessions and leave your family, you're not off the hook. I'm not either. **The choice of following Him is still ours to make on a daily basis.** I constantly struggle with the quality of my commitment to follow Jesus. Even though I'm committed to be His follower, and put Him first by living His way, I still have my own tendency to put me first and live my way. Are you in the same camp? I've talked to a lot of people who want to follow Christ as long as it leads them to big contracts, top grades, the best jobs, no pressures at home, etc. Are you that way?

It's easy to kid ourselves, isn't it? We say we love Jesus but we still get caught up in all the little things around us. For instance, we know God wants us to know His word thoroughly (2 Timothy 2:15). But even a boring TV program will often take priority over reading the Bible. It's much easier to "vegetate" in front of the TV than it is to learn from God's word. I'm not saying TV is wrong, but we need to examine ourselves and see if our TV is taking priority over God.

Another good example of how we kid ourselves is what we do when a guy cuts in front of us on the highway. Even though we know God wants us to be at peace with all men, so far as it depends on us (Romans 12:18), it's far easier to get revenge by laying on the horn. So, what's our problem? It all

comes down to this. **We don't really love Jesus Christ as much as we think we do or even want to.** At that moment, we actually love ourselves more! Here's a good yardstick by which we can measure just how much we really love Jesus.

LOVE PRODUCES ACTION

> "If you **love** Me, you will **keep** My commandments. And I will ask the Father, and He will give you another **Helper,** that He may be with you forever..."
>
> John 14:15-16

These are the words of Jesus. And He didn't pull any punches, did He? He came right to the point. **Love for Him results in my obeying Him.** Are you consciously obeying Jesus Christ? I don't mean are you living a life free from any glaring mistakes? But are you obeying Him in getting along with your neighbor, raising your children the way He wants you to, loving your mate? Chances are you generally do what you think He wants you to do, but how about the specifics? Are you aware of His specific instructions to you in these various areas of responsibility? For instance, could you list five attitudes He wants you to have while you work?

Most of our obedience to Jesus is pretty shallow, isn't it? We haven't taken time to consider what He has to say about the various situations we're involved in each day. So, do we really love Him as much as we'd like to think we do? An all-out commitment to Jesus will result in attitudes and actions that are pleasing to Him. If my love isn't there, I can't expect Christ-like attitudes and actions to be either. **Without loving Him I can talk His talk, but I can't walk His walk!**

John, a close friend of Jesus, caught the meaning of this when he wrote, "...the one who says he abides in Him ought himself to walk in the same manner as He walked" (1 John 2:6). "Abides" implies a togetherness. It describes a committed Christian's relationship with Jesus. In other words, if you say you're a follower of Jesus Christ, then you ought to be thinking and doing those things He'd do. But, before you can pattern your life after Him, you must learn His ways. Then, as you commit your will to follow Him and His ways, the Holy Spirit is there to help you. **The degree to which you purposely do what's pleasing to Jesus reveals how much you really love Him!** That's true of any love relationship, isn't it?

For instance, a girl I once dated liked me to open doors for her. And, I did every now and then, but never enough to please her. When I met my wife to be, I discovered she also enjoyed having me open doors for her. As our romance developed, and our love grew, I found myself opening doors for her every opportunity I could get. I still do to this day! I want to do things pleasing to my wife because I love her. Now, I don't do it because I'm a compulsive door opener or because she demands it. I don't do it when I find it convenient, or when I feel like it. **I do it because I want to show my love for her in this simple, tangible way.** That's what real everyday love is all about! A commitment to do things for the benefit of another person in spite of personal sacrifice. Love really does produce action!

We can also see that truth through biblical history. One day when David, the greatest king in Israel's history, was camping with his troops, three of his men from another camp came to talk to him. These were three of his highest ranking officers who had been with him a long time. As they talked about old times, David must have reminisced about the great taste of water from a well in his home town of Bethlehem. Because the well was in enemy hands, David hadn't tasted this water for quite some time.

As time passed after their visit, who should reappear with a pitcher of water, but David's three friends. The Bible tells us they broke through enemy lines to get that water from the well in Bethlehem. Why did they risk their lives? Was it because David was thirsty? No! A great leader like David wouldn't camp without water. He had water but not from the well in Bethlehem. **Getting that water was his friends' way of showing how much they really loved him.** Their love for David produced a sacrificial action. And that action was their expression of love!

How much do you really love Jesus? What are you purposely doing to show your love for Him? Are you consciously lining your thoughts up with Christ's throughout the day? Do you bring your attitudes and actions in line with His regardless of personal sacrifices? It's a sobering thought to know **our actions reveal the quality of our love for Him**, isn't it?

We've seen, in the last chapter, how much God loves us. Think about what His Son really went through to demonstrate the quality of His love for us. We have an opportunity to commit ourselves, moment by moment throughout the day, to express the quality of our love for Him through our attitudes, thoughts and actions. What fantastic days we can live when this becomes our **motivation** in everything we do!

FOR INDEPENDENT AND GROUP STUDY

1. How would you describe your love for Jesus? As an all-out love, warm at times or fairly cold? Give reasons for your answer.

2. What would your response be if Jesus actually did ask you to follow Him and leave your family behind?

3. Can you remember a situation in your life when your love for someone was the motivation for doing things to please that person? If so, please explain.

4. What are some ways you can specifically express your love for Jesus as you relate to another person?

"BE DILIGENT TO PRESENT YOURSELF APPROVED TO GOD AS A WORKMAN WHO DOES NOT NEED TO BE ASHAMED, HANDLING ACCURATELY THE WORD OF TRUTH."

2 Timothy 2:15

CHAPTER SEVEN

YOUR INCREDIBLE PARTNERSHIP

For centuries Christians have wanted the secret for living the Christian life. Formulas after formulas have evolved to shed light on it. But no formula has been quite so simple and effective as Jesus Christ's own words, "If you love Me, you will keep My commandments. And I will ask the Father, and He will give you another Helper, that He may be with you forever..." (John 14:15-16).

"Helper" here refers to the Holy Spirit who indwells every Christian just as Jesus said He would (1 Corinthians 3:16). **One of the Holy Spirit's main roles is to help us carry out the commandments of Jesus.** He does this as we consciously commit our will to keep Jesus' commandments as an expression of our love for Him. Here then, in a nutshell, is how God has designed the Christian life to be lived as we aim at patterning our lives after Jesus Christ.

> **As we actively express our love to Jesus Christ by keeping His commandments, the Holy Spirit will give us His power to keep them and enable us to live the Christian life the way God intended.**

Sounds simple, doesn't it? It is, in theory. But, before we can keep His commandments, we must not only know them, but we must also understand how to apply them to our daily situations. And, that takes time. The better we get to know Jesus and His ways, the easier it'll be to know what He'd do in our shoes.

In this chapter I'll try to deal with a few of the more frequently asked questions concerning this approach to living the Christian life. Hopefully, you'll get a better understanding of how God has designed your life to be lived. Then, I believe you'll become more impressed, than ever before, with the incredible partnership you have with God, Himself.

1. You emphasize keeping the commandments of Jesus as an expression of our love for Him. What about the rest of God's word? Are we to pay equal attention to the writings of the Old Testament as well as the teachings of Paul, James, Peter and John?

Yes. When Jesus tells us we'll keep His commandments as an expression of our love for Him, He's implying **we're to keep all of God's word.** The Bible clearly tells us Jesus is the focus of both the Old and New Testaments. For instance, He created all things (Hebrews 1:2-3), is the same as His Father (John 8:58, John 10:30 and Revelation 1:8), and He's made known the invisible God to us (John 1:18). Although His life communicates God's total revelation to us, Jesus, Himself, taught that man shouldn't live by bread alone but by **every word** that comes out of the mouth of God (Matthew 4:4). This includes all of God's word. I believe as we understand more of the entire Bible, we'll understand more of Jesus Christ. And, as we obey all of God's word, we're obeying Jesus Christ.

2. I get the impression that keeping Jesus' commandments is a willful, self-effort and is something I've got to do by my own power. Is this true?

Fortunately, this isn't so. The Christian life is a supernatural life and can't be lived by natural means. I can't live it by my own power alone anymore than I can lift a 3500 pound car overhead by using only my own power. The instant you became a Christian, God sent His Spirit to indwell you. The Holy Spirit is supernatural and it's only by His power you can live the Christian life!

> "...that He would grant you, according to the riches of His glory, to be strengthened with power through His Spirit in the inner man..."
>
> Ephesians 3:16

The Christian life does require much effort on your part, but the Holy Spirit gives you His power to make that effort. To try and live the Christian life apart from the Holy Spirit's power would be as practical as trying to make an electric refrigerator run without plugging it into a source of electrical power. **A supernatural life requires a supernatural power source!** So, as we express our love to Jesus by keeping His commandments, it's not by our own power. The Holy Spirit is our Helper, giving us His power to do what's pleasing to Jesus. You might say when we make the effort to do things

God's way, we trigger the "switch" that releases the Holy Spirit's power in our lives.

3. I'm confused about the command in Ephesians 5:18 to "be filled with the Spirit." How does this relate to your emphasis on living the Christian life by keeping the commands of Jesus as an expression of our love for Him?

Paul uses the term "filled" in Ephesians 5:18 to describe the filling of something with absolutely no room for anything else. You'll notice his preceding statement is a command not to be drunk with wine. Paul is pointing out that a drunk person's mind would be under the influence of the wine. And, his actions would reveal that influence. So, when Paul commanded the believers to be filled with the Spirit, rather than be drunk with wine, **he commanded them to have their minds totally influenced at all times by the Spirit of God.** As a result, their actions would reveal the Holy Spirit's influence just as a drunk person's actions would reveal the wine's influence.

That's why Paul follows this command to be filled with the Spirit with several actions to indicate whether the believer really is filled. If he's filled, he'll be speaking to other people in psalms, hymns and spiritual songs. In other words, he'll be talking to people from God's perspective. He'll also be giving thanks for all things and subjecting himself to other people. It's interesting that Paul also described these same actions in Colossians 3:16. But instead of commanding the Colossians to be "filled with the Spirit," as he did the Ephesians, he commanded them to "Let the word of Christ richly dwell within you..." Bible scholars tell us that Paul wrote both letters during the same week from his quarters in a Roman prison. And, using different words, he told both groups of Christians to do the same thing. **To be filled with the Spirit is to have Christ's words so much at home in you that you're putting them into practice.** Your attitudes, thoughts and actions will have a Christ-likeness.

4. But, aren't I living a life pleasing to God as long as the Holy Spirit doesn't convict me of any sin? In other words, can I assume I'm filled with the Spirit as long as I don't feel convicted by Him?

Unfortunately, we can't assume the Holy Spirit is filling us just because He hasn't convicted us of any sin. One of the problems that has arisen during the last few years is the idea the Holy Spirit convicts the believer of sin independently of

God's word. If He did, then it would be good logic to assume we'd be filled with the Spirit unless He convicts us of sin. Perhaps one of the reasons this thought has developed is the words of Jesus, "And He [Holy Spirit], when He comes, will convict the world concerning sin, and righteousness, and judgment..." (John 16:8).

It almost sounds like Jesus could mean the Holy Spirit will convict the believer of sin, doesn't it? But the context gives us a different meaning. Jesus continued, "...concerning sin, because they do not believe in Me..." (John 16:9). You see, Jesus was speaking about the nonbelieving world, not His own followers. **No where in the Bible does God tell us the Holy Spirit convicts the believer of sin independently of God's word.**

A well known California minister once shared a story of what happened when he went to Hawaii to perform a wedding. The Christian couple asking him to officiate had been living together for quite awhile and wanted him to make it official. "This is fantastic!" exclaimed the minister. "It's so great you understand you've been living in sin and now want to make it right before God!" "What do you mean?" asked the man. "We haven't been living in sin!"

"Sure you have," replied the minister. "God's word is pretty clear on it." The man turned to the woman and asked her if she knew they were living in sin. She didn't either.

Somehow, neither of them knew that to live together in a sexual union outside of marriage was wrong from God's perspective. Although these two people were Christians, the Holy Spirit hadn't convicted them of their sin because they didn't know what God's word had to say about it. Now, I know this sounds far-fetched. You'd think any Christian would know a sexual relationship outside of marriage was wrong from God's perspective. But it did happen! I believe this couple was a product of the culture around them. Without God's word they didn't have knowledge of God's values. The Holy Spirit didn't convict them independently of God's word.

Just as a sword was one of the offensive weapons used in Paul's day, the word of God is the Holy Spirit's offensive weapon to help cut sin away from a Christian. That's why Paul described the word of God as a sword when he wrote, "And take the helmet of salvation, and the sword of the Spirit, which is the word of God" (Ephesians 6:17). It wasn't until the minister showed the young couple, from the Bible, what God had to say about their situation that they felt any conviction from the Holy Spirit. It was the offensive, cutting power from God's word that the Spirit used.

> "For the word of God is living and active and sharper than any two-edged sword, and piercing as far as the division of soul and spirit, of both joints and marrow, and able to judge the thoughts and intentions of the heart."
>
> Hebrews 4:12

The danger I see in thinking we're convicted of sin by the Holy Spirit, independently of God's word, is we can get lazy in keeping God's thoughts and ways first in our minds. That was a problem with the couple in Hawaii. They were trying to live the Christian life based on a naturalistic culture in which they lived. But, God wants us to fill our minds with His word which creates for us His new culture. We can wrongly think we're under the Spirit's influence just because we've asked Him to fill us at some time.

5. Then are you saying a Christian isn't filled by the Holy Spirit simply by asking?

That's right. It would be great if it was that simple. But I don't believe the Bible supports that approach. Let's get an

understanding about how this approach of asking to be filled with the Spirit developed. It's built primarily upon two biblical passages:

> "...be filled with the Spirit..."
>
> Ephesians 5:18

> "And this is the confidence which we have before Him, that, if we ask anything according to His will, He hears us! And if we know that He hears us in whatever we ask, we know that we have the requests which we have asked from Him."
>
> 1 John 5:14-15

The logic behind asking to be filled with the Spirit goes this way. Since we know God desires us to be filled with His Spirit (Ephesians 5:18), and since God tells us we have anything we ask as long as it's His will (1 John 5:14-15), then it stands to reason all we have to do is ask for the filling. **But the logic breaks down as we begin to put these two passages into a correct perspective.** Let's quickly explore five of these areas where I believe the logic breaks down.

A. If 1 John 5:14-15 is valid for asking to be filled with the Spirit, then why can't we ask God for anything He has commanded us and expect it to immediately happen? For instance, there are over 600 commands in the New Testament alone. One of them tells me I should love my wife as Christ loved the church (Ephesians 5:25). Another one tells me to set my mind on things above and not on the things on earth (Colossians 3:2). Can I love my wife as Christ loved the church, and keep my mind on things above, simply by asking God to make these things happen? It doesn't happen that way, does it?

You see, God gives commands because we don't naturally do them. Anytime we see a command in the Bible, we have a responsibility to respond to it. If God intended us simply to ask Him to make it a reality, I believe He would have made that clear in His word. He could have listed all of His desires for us and then told us to ask Him to make them real in our lives. But He didn't do it that way! **We must willfully choose to live God's way.** That's why the Helper is there to come alongside and help us after we've chosen to go God's way in a situation.

B. God's command for us to be filled with the Spirit (Ephesians 5:18) is written in the **present** tense. This means He desires us to be **continuously filled** with the Spirit, not just occasionally. If the command to be continuously filled is accomplished simply by asking, then we'd **never** experience a time when we aren't filled. But, we experience many times when we aren't filled, don't we? Our lives show our attitudes, thoughts and actions aren't what God wants them to be much of the time.

C. The command to be filled, in Ephesians 5:18, was written by **Paul** in about **AD 61**. However, the passage used as the premise to ask for the filling, in 1 John 5:14-15, was written by the apostle **John** in about **AD 91**. If Paul gave us the command to be filled, why didn't he also give us the formula for being filled? Why was this formula written 30 years after the command was given? And, what were the Christians supposed to do in the meantime in order to be filled?

D. One of the most notorious churches for ungodly behavior was the Corinthian Church. Why didn't Paul command the Corinthians to be filled with the Spirit in either of his two long letters to them? That would have solved their problems. **Well, he really did, but not in those words.** You see, if the Corinthians carried out all of Paul's instructions for godly living, they would have been filled with the Holy Spirit.

E. Finally, if God intended the filling to take place simply by our asking, why wasn't the command in Ephesians 5:18 to

ask for the filling? It says to **be** filled, not to ask for it. Whenever I tell my two little girls to do something, I don't expect them to turn around and ask me if they can do it. **Anytime a command is given, a response is expected.** And, the response Paul expected from his readers was that of allowing the Holy Spirit to work through them as they focused their attention on doing what was pleasing to God.

6. If 1 John 5:14-15 can't be applied to asking for the filling of the Spirit, why does God tell us we can have anything we ask as long as it's according to His will?

Whenever we try to grasp the meaning of a certain passage in the Bible, we've got to understand the context in which it was written. One of the basic rules in interpreting God's word is a passage must always be interpreted in light of other passages. So, in order to get a better understanding of what John meant in 1 John 5:14-15, let's look at what he wrote earlier in that same letter.

> "...and whatever we ask we receive from Him, because **we keep His commandments** and do the things that are pleasing in His sight."
>
> 1 John 3:22

You'll notice John wrote about receiving what we ask from God in this passage just as he did later in 1 John 5:14-15. But here the emphasis is on obedience. As long as we're deliberately keeping His commandments, and doing things pleasing to God, we can expect to have those things we ask of Him. Doesn't it also stand to reason that the closer the companionship we have with Jesus, the more our requests will be the ones He wants us to make?

John wasn't writing a formula on how to be filled with the Spirit in 1 John 5:14-15. **He was writing to Christians who were already filled with the Spirit because of their obedience to God.** I believe he wrote 1 John 5:14-15 to encourage Christians to make sure their requests in prayer lined up with God's desires for them, rather than with their own independent, personal desires.

7. I've asked to be filled with the Spirit before and have felt close to God when I did. After asking, I've also seen changes in my life, like more effective witnessing for Jesus and more love for others. How do you account for this?

Most likely when you asked to be filled with the Holy Spirit you were expressing a desire to live a life that was pleasing to God. That desire to please Him could have made you feel closer to Him. Too, you were being obedient by making your requests known to God (Philippians 4:6). God often gives us a sense of His presence when we set our will on doing those things pleasing to Him.

As far as the changes you experienced in your life, could they have been because you were determined to make your life count more for Him? Witnessing for Jesus and loving others are things God desires us to do. As you set your will to do them, the Helper made them a reality in your life. So then, it wasn't the "asking" that made the changes, but the Holy Spirit empowering you as you set out to do what was pleasing to God. **It was your willful obedience that freed the Spirit to make them a reality.**

I'm sure you still have things in your life you'd like to have changed, don't you? Well, the Holy Spirit hasn't failed you in them. It'll just take a commitment on your part to begin doing things God's way in those areas. Then you'll experience the Holy Spirit making the necessary changes.

8. What's the main danger in asking to be filled with the Spirit?

I believe the main danger in asking to be filled with the Spirit is in thinking you're living a life pleasing to God, when in reality you might not be. It's easy to be lulled into a life of passiveness as far as our responsibility goes. **By believing we're filled simply by asking, we can get the idea that whatever we do, after asking, is automatically God's will.** But our experience shows we don't automatically do things God's way. By asking to be filled, it's easy to forget about the responsibility we have to search out His ways. And, over 600 commands in the New Testament alone point out we certainly do have a responsibility!

9. What's my responsibility in living the Christian life?

Whenever we use the word responsibility we usually attach work to it. And, there's work involved in living the Christian life! Jesus summed up our responsibility by saying, "If you love Me, you will keep My commandments. And I will ask the Father, and He will give you another Helper, that He may be with you forever" (John 14:15-16). **Our responsibility is to come to love Jesus, and then obey Him as an ex-**

pression of that love. We can't fulfill our responsibility without knowing how the word of God applies to our specific situations.

That's why the psalmist wrote, "Wherewith shall a young man cleanse his way? By taking heed and keeping watch [on himself] according to Your word [conforming his life to it]. With my whole heart have I sought You, inquiring for and of You, and yearning for You; O let me not wander or step aside [either in ignorance or willfully] from Your commandments" (Psalms 119:9-10, The Amplified Bible). It's not a matter of just getting into God's word, but getting God's word into us.

10. But, can't obedience be overdone and border on legalism?

It all depends on our motivation. Legalism is doing something to win someone else's approval. The obedience I'm talking about is an expression of our love for Jesus. It's doing something because we want to please Him. You see, legalism is **self-oriented** and it's done for our own benefit. On the other hand, obedience, as a love expression to Jesus, is **Jesus-oriented** and it's done for His benefit. Now, we're secure in Jesus' love whether we obey Him or not. We're not trying to please Him to chalk up spiritual points. We only want to please Him because we love Him and want to show our love by doing what He asks. **And, He's already told us that obedience to Him is how He wants us to express our love for Him.**

Let's say one of my girls came to me and said, "Daddy, I'm gonna put my bike away everyday just like you want me to." Wouldn't I be foolish to say, "Hey, don't do that. That's legalistic!" And, what if she replied, "Daddy, I don't know what 'legalistic' means. I just want to do it because I love you and know it'll please you." That's not legalism anymore, is it? She'd be obeying me as an expression of her love for me. And, that's our responsibility in the Christian life! First, to **love** Jesus with all of our hearts, and then to **obey** Him as an expression of that love!

The Christian life can't be lived apart from us carrying out our responsibility, nor can it be lived apart from the Holy Spirit's power. **What an incredible partnership we have!**

PART TWO

BIBLICAL HANDLES FOR LIVING THE CHRISTIAN LIFE

CHAPTER EIGHT

THE FIVE "S" MENTAL APPROACH

How well I remember a February morning I was supposed to take our kindergartner to the school bus stop. It was one of those rushed mornings, and I had the time of leaving the house scheduled without a second to spare. As I dashed out the front door, with my daughter's hand in mine, I quickly noticed a thick coating of frost on the truck windshield. I hadn't planned on that! There was no way I could drive the half mile to the bus stop without first defrosting the windshield. So, with tension building I rushed back up the front stairs to get a pitcher of lukewarm water to douse on the windshield. Coming down the stairs I knew it was a lost cause, that we would miss the bus. What a way to start the morning. Sabotaged by Jack Frost!

I was irritated, upset, bent out of shape. Whatever you want to call it! But fortunately I didn't stay that way for long. As I walked to the truck with the pitcher in hand one word came to my mind, followed by four others, that gave me a new outlook. As I considered the five words, my heart beat slower and I actually enjoyed defrosting the windshield. What was the first word that started me thinking differently? Significance!

It's the first of five words, each beginning with the letter "S", that help me see things God's way as I face various, and sometimes difficult, situations each day. The five words are Significance, Strategy, Singularity, Sacrifice and Sovereignty. Let's look at each word and see how they changed my outlook that morning and how they can help you see your daily situations from God's viewpoint.

1. SIGNIFICANCE. The significant thing about every situation is you're a personal ambassador for Jesus Christ.

> "Therefore, we are **ambassadors for Christ**, as though God were entreating through us..."
>
> 2 Corinthians 5:20

Remember, you're an ambassador for Jesus Christ.

As you know, an ambassador is someone who represents another person. His main responsibility is to carry out the will of the one he represents, rather than do things his own way. The same is true with us as ambassadors for Jesus Christ. **We must be committed to do exactly what pleases Jesus in every situation, rather than do things our own natural way.** Even when we're inconvenienced, or it looks like we're going to lose the contract, or when we have unexpected visitors and the house is in shambles, etc. Our first responsibility is to be ambassadors for Jesus Christ. As significant as those other things are, they aren't as significant as us being Christ-like in dealing with them.

When the word Significance came to my mind that icy morning, I was reminded of my responsibility to be Jesus

Christ's personal ambassador in getting my little girl to school. But how would I represent Him? That question brought the second word beginning with "S" to my mind -- Strategy.

2. STRATEGY. Since you're Christ's personal ambassador in everything you do, it's highly important you understand the strategy of how He would do things.

> "And whatever you do in word or deed, do all in the name of the Lord Jesus..."
>
> Colossians 3:17

Think through what Jesus would do.

"In the name of" means you do things just as Jesus Christ would in your situation. That's what your strategy is. **Strategy asks, "What would Jesus do now?"** Of course, the more we saturate our minds with God's word, the easier that answer will come. Then, we'll be quicker to relate His attitudes, thoughts and actions to our particular situations.

Well, that February morning, I wondered how Jesus would handle my situation. I knew there was no way we could get to the bus stop on time, and from my initial perspective, I thought the 20 minutes it would take to drive to school would put tremendous pressure on an already heavily scheduled day. I just couldn't see any good that could come from my predicament. But as I tried to think of what Jesus would do, I recalled the day when Jesus received "bad news" of His friend Lazarus being very sick (John 11:1-16). In fact, He knew Lazarus would die from the sickness. His disciples couldn't understand why Jesus insisted on staying where they were a couple of days longer instead of immediately going to see their dying friend. It wasn't until Jesus raised Lazarus from the dead they realized this initial "bad news" and Jesus' delay in going to Lazarus was necessary.

Just as Lazarus had to die in order for God's perfect plan to be worked out, I realized I could miss a school bus and God could still work everything together for His good. That situation Jesus was in helped me see what my strategy in representing Him should be. I needed to keep thinking that God would work everything out for His best interests. And, as Christ's personal ambassador, His best interests would be mine. Once I knew how Jesus would handle it, I thought of the third word beginning with "S" -- Singularity.

3. SINGULARITY. Every minute of everything you do is the single most important minute you have because you'll never have that particular minute to live again.

> "Therefore be careful how you walk, not as unwise men, but as wise, **making the most of your time,** because the days are evil."
>
> Ephesians 5:15-16

"Making the most of your time" is using every minute exactly as Jesus would. This challenge from the apostle Paul was something he took very seriously himself. Sure he had those lapse moments, just as we do, but he always tried to keep his mind active in representing Jesus Christ. And, God used him greatly in the midst of very evil days.

How I dealt with my inconvenience of missing the bus would be recorded in eternity as well as in the mind of my daughter. I'd never have those moments to relive. I needed to see each moment of that situation as an opportunity to live by Jesus' attitudes and ways instead of give into my natural tendency of being irritated.

Your actions and thoughts count for eternity.

Now, is it really possible to use every minute just as Jesus would? A national champion wrestler seemed to think so, and one day he revealed how he did it in his wrestling matches. He said he broke down the eight minutes a wrestling match has into 480 one-second periods. Then he concentrated on giving 100% of himself during each of those one-second periods just as Jesus did in each situation throughout His life. That's a graphic example of what it means to make the most of your time applying it to one situation at a time!

Now, I'm not saying we can arrive at 100% perfection in using every minute just as Jesus would. That would mean we'd be perfect, a condition that won't be ours until we're with Him in heaven. But, God wants us to work toward that perfection now (Matthew 5:48), and consider every minute of the day as important to Him, and to us for all eternity! **He wants us to take every thought captive to Jesus (2 Corinthians 10:5).** We have a difficult time with this, don't we? Because it's difficult for us to understand how it's done, we tend to be doubtful. But, let's remember we have within us the Holy Spirit, who will help make it happen as we work at bringing each thought under Jesus' control.

When you take Singularity into consideration, nothing is really routine anymore, is it? Thirty minutes of doing the dishes can be broken down into 1800 one-second periods. The five minutes it takes to feed the dogs can be broken down into 300 one-second periods. You get the point. You'll never have any of those seconds to relive. Once I considered that I'd never be able to relive those exact moments of defrosting the windshield, and driving my daughter the few miles to school, I wanted those moments to count for eternity. That's when I committed myself to carry out the strategy of Jesus in relying on God to work out His plan. Then came the fourth word beginning with "S" -- Sacrifice -- which helped reinforce that commitment.

4. SACRIFICE. Sacrifice is committing yourself to do what God most desires for you rather than doing what you most desire for yourself. It's dying to what you want to do and living for what Jesus would do.

It's what Jesus wants you to do that counts.

The apostle Paul put it this way:

> "I have been crucified with Christ; and **it is no longer I who live,** but Christ lives in me..."
>
> Galatians 2:20

One of the most remarkable examples of this type of sacrifice, that comes to my mind, is a man nicknamed "Holy Hubert." This colorfully clad man has become a legend in preaching the good news of Jesus Christ to students as they pass on the sidewalks bordering the University of California in Berkeley. I saw him there during the turbulent "Free Speech" era of the mid-1960s. During this time he had been shot and stabbed on several occasions. But, in spite of his narrow escapes from death he continued to return and boldly speak out his biblical message. Once when he was asked, "Aren't you afraid for your life?" he replied, "No. You see, I'm a dead man in Jesus Christ and a dead man has nothing to fear." That's the real meaning of Sacrifice. **We have to see ourselves as "dead" to our own natural ways, in order to be totally alive to do what Jesus wants us to do.**

What a different picture I had of my "negative" circumstances when I became "dead" to my desire to keep my schedule intact, and alive to how God would work it out for His purpose. After I let go of my own desires, I was ready to think about the fifth word beginning with "S" -- Sovereignty.

5. SOVEREIGNTY. God is sovereign and He either allows or causes all things to happen. If He didn't, He'd be less than God.

> "And we know that God causes **all things** to work together for good to those who love God, to those who are called according to His purpose."
>
> Romans 8:28

"All things" even includes a frosted windshield. Although I realized I needed to plan better the next morning, **I was able to have peace even in the midst of unpleasant circumstances caused by my poor planning that morning.** I couldn't make the bus wait for us. But God could have, if He wanted. Nothing is impossible for Him! So, with this in mind I accepted my situation and directed my attention on having a good time relating to my daughter on our drive to school.

God either causes or allows all things to happen.

It's never fun to have circumstances go wrong, is it? A contract doesn't materialize. The drain clogs up. You don't get the date. Your dinner is burned. And, a bus is missed! **But, God's promise, in Romans 8:28, gives us confidence He'll work out each situation to His good if we're loving Him.** And, we're loving Him if we're willfully doing what pleases Him (John 14:15). Yes, He'll work it out for good. And, good it was as I drove my little girl into town. We sang songs, laughed and really enjoyed each other. God worked my "interruption" into a "date" with my daughter. And, I found it was easier than I at first thought to rearrange my day's schedule.

So, as you encounter each situation, remember: The **significant** thing about that situation is you're to represent Jesus Christ in it. Then, look for what **strategy** He would have. Ask yourself, "What would Jesus do, now?" Keep in mind, the **singularity** of the moment. It is the most important moment you have for eternity, because it can never be relived. **Sacrifice** what you naturally would want to do in favor of what you think Jesus would do. And, realize God is totally **sovereign.** He'll bring about the results He wants.

This thought sequence can take place in seconds and turn a situation that would ordinarily be upsetting, into a situation in which you're totally at peace. A natural question you might have is, "But how do you bring yourself to think of the Five "S" Mental Approach when you're in the middle of a testing situation?"

TRAINING YOUR MIND

These five words, beginning with "S", are simply reminders of what it means to follow more closely in the steps of Jesus Christ. I was able to recall them easily that frost-bit morning only because I had already riveted them in my mind and trained myself to use them. It won't happen automatically with you either. It'll take some effort on your part just as it did for me. Here are two easy steps I took in getting them in my mind.

1. Memorize the five words and their meanings. Remove the Five "S" tear-out pages, in the back of this book, and place them in convenient locations. Then, everytime you see them, they'll be reinforced in your mind. You'll want to learn the definition of each word so well, you'll be able to explain them to someone else.

2. Select something you'll be doing each day for the next five days. Then, each day talk to God about what you selected using the Five "S" sequence. Here's an example of how to do it. Let's say on one of the days you have to confront an employee concerning a lazy attitude. Your conversation with God concerning that meeting with your employee might go something like this.

SIGNIFICANCE. "Father, I know it's more significant that I represent Your Son accurately in talking with Tom than it is in how Tom responds to me. That's good for me to keep in mind. I actually am Jesus Christ's personal ambassador to Tom."

STRATEGY. "I really want to talk to Tom the way Jesus would. Father, I don't know why Tom is so lazy. Maybe it's because he never had a good concept of himself. But, I know Your Son understood His disciples' weaknesses even when they let Him down by falling asleep in the Garden of Gethsemane. Yet, even though He understood, He still rebuked them. From that I can see I need to try to understand why Tom has his lazy attitude, but that I still need to correct him on it."

SINGULARITY. "I know I'll never have a chance to relive today's talk with Tom. Father, I want to make every second count for eternity by accurately representing Jesus in the way I try to understand Tom as well as correct him."

SACRIFICE. "You know, Father, my natural tendency is to be really upset with Tom. I've never been able to stand a lazy person! But, I'm going to sacrifice my desire to tell him off for Your way of trying to understand him more. I'm grateful Your Holy Spirit will be there to help me understand him as well as correct him, so Tom can reach his full potential."

SOVEREIGNTY. "I know you'll bring about the results You want in my conversation with Tom. He may or may not change. You've promised to work situations like this together for good to those who love You and are called according to Your purpose. So, I'll accept whatever You allow or cause. Just knowing You're in control really frees me to do what I know Jesus would do without trying to manipulate what results I want."

USING THE FIVE "S" MENTAL APPROACH

Sometimes it's helpful to go through the entire sequence when you're in a situation, as we just did. Other times, when you're in a particular situation, just one of the words might come to your mind. For instance, you can train your mind to remember "Sovereignty" every time you feel frustrated or receive bad news. Your frustration and disappointment will soon leave because you know God either causes or allows all things to happen, and He's in control of the situation.

Five words, each beginning with the letter "S", each representing a vital biblical principle! As they become more a part of how you deal with daily situations, you'll experience being able to follow more closely in the steps of Jesus. And, the Holy Spirit will be transforming you more into Christlikeness!

FOR INDEPENDENT AND GROUP STUDY

1. Why should you memorize the Five "S" Mental Approach?

2. If you haven't done so already, memorize the five words, along with their definitions.

3. Choose one difficult situation from your job and another from your home life. Then, taking each situation separately, write down how you would handle each one using the Five "S" Mental Approach.

"SET YOUR MIND ON THE THINGS ABOVE, NOT ON THE THINGS THAT ARE ON EARTH. FOR YOU HAVE DIED AND YOUR LIFE IS HIDDEN WITH CHRIST IN GOD."

Colossians 3:2-3

CHAPTER NINE

FOCAL POINTS

"That's easier said than done," thought Susan as she listened to the sermon. After the service, when she was walking out, she wondered how many of the listeners would really remember to do the things the minister talked about. On their drive home she asked her husband, "Ron, do you have a hard time remembering what God wants you to do?"

"Huh? Oh yeah. I guess so. Why?" "Well, we both want to do things God's way, don't we?" Susan asked. "Sure!" replied Ron. "But we usually end up doing things our own way." "That's what I was thinking," said Susan. "I wonder if that'll always be true. I get so disappointed."

As she was talking, they drove by a park where a man was instructing a group of young boys how to play football. "Wouldn't it be great," Ron mused, "if we had someone constantly coaching us to do things God's way?"

SELF EVALUATION

1. How much of the time do you think your attitudes, thoughts and actions are pleasing to God?

☐ Majority of the time

☐ About half of the time

☐ Hardly ever

2. Would it help if you were reminded how God wanted you to do things during the day?

☐ Very much

☐ Sometimes

☐ Very little

IT'S OUR RESPONSIBILITY

Ron's idea of having a personal coach to remind him how to live the Christian life throughout each day isn't bad, is it? Many Christians mistakenly have the impression it's the Holy Spirit who automatically does the "coaching." But, as we've already seen in Chapter Six, the Bible teaches that the Holy Spirit helps us do those things pleasing to Jesus as we commit our will to do them. Jesus said, "If you love Me, you will keep My commandments. And I will ask the Father, and He will give you another Helper, that He may be with you forever..." (John 14:15-16). "You will keep My commandments" indicates **we're responsible to coach ourselves throughout each day.** Then, after we willfully commit ourselves to do something God's way, the Holy Spirit will help us do it.

OUR PROBLEM

Now, we all experience times when we purposely disobey God. For instance, we know it's wrong to drive faster than the legal speed limit. But, we sometimes do it anyway. That's our choice, and it's wrong! Most of the time, however, we don't fall short of God's way because we choose to do it, but because **we get so wrapped up in other things.** Getting the dinner ready. Planning for business. Preparing for a meeting. Reacting to the guy who just cut in front of us on the freeway. Watching a television show. Because we easily get absorbed in other things, God commanded us to keep our minds focused on things above, or of the Lord, rather than things on the earth (Colossians 3:2). But, it's neither easy, nor natural, to keep in mind how Jesus would have us get dinner, plan for business or react to the "careless" driver in front of us on the freeway. We're naturally lazy in doing this.

GOD HAS GIVEN US A SOLUTION

Well, relax. Lazily neglecting God's way isn't new with His people. It was the same story with the people of Israel throughout Old Testament history. They'd get so caught up in doing things their own way, that they'd frequently forget what would be pleasing to God. That's why, in Numbers 15:37-41, God gave Moses specific instructions as to how the people of Israel should be reminded to please Him.

God told His people to attach a tassel to their garments with a blue cord, so everytime they saw the tassel they'd be reminded of how great God is and what He'd done for them. **The idea was they'd then remember to carry out God's instructions to them instead of follow after their own hearts.** Sounds pretty practical, doesn't it?

Well, the principle remains just as helpful today as it did then. Now, don't panic! You don't have to go out and buy tassels to tie on your clothes. But, how about taking a little time to consider some situations, or objects, that'll help remind you of God's way of doing things? Instead of tassels, let's call these reminders to live God's way, **focal points.** A focal point is a situation, or object, that can be used to focus our attention on God and His way of doing things.

These focal points can be either tangible or intangible. For example, one of my tangible focal points is a mirror. Everytime I look into one, I'm reminded of God telling me I'm a personal ambassador for Jesus Christ (2 Corinthians 5:20). So, as I look at the mirror to shave each morning, I'm reminded I'm to represent Jesus throughout the day. Then, I try to think of what that means in representing Him to my wife and children. I also think through various situations I'll face at work, as well as at home. I want people to see in me the reflection of the One I follow.

Another type of tangible focal point can be the intersection where roads meet. I heard of a man who remembered how much God loved Him everytime he came to an intersection. It reminded him of the cross and how much pain Jesus endured to demonstrate God's love.

An example of an intangible focal point can be the countenance of a person, or the inflection of a person's voice. For instance, everytime you see someone depressed you can be reminded of God telling you to speak only words that'll give comfort and encouragement to the person (Ephesians 4:29). When you hear a harsh or angry voice, it can remind you to respond God's way with a gentle and diplomatic answer (Proverbs 15:1).

HOW TO GET STARTED

Now, all this won't happen without your effort. Just seeing, or hearing, a focal point won't automatically produce God's way in you. **You've still got to willfully do what the focal point reminds you to do.** So, it'll take a commitment on your part! And, it'll take time to train yourself to immediately do things God's way in each situation.

A good place to start in developing focal points is the life of Jesus Christ. You'll find, at the end of each analyzation of His life in this book, a suggested focal point with an accompanying Christ-like response. A helpful way to rivet them into your mind is to copy them onto a 3 x 5 card. Then, place the card somewhere you'll see it throughout the day. Everytime you see the card, try to think of a situation where you can apply it. For example, if one of your copied down focal points was Handling Difficult Circumstances, you might apply it to a machine that broke down one day. On another day, you might apply it to your proposed plan that was rejected. In both situations, you'd realize that God's purpose will be carried out because of the broken down machine and rejected plan, or in spite of them. Then, you'd be able to deal with both situations without being angered or stymied.

To help you get started, you'll find some focal points and Christ-like responses printed on some of the **tear-out pages** in the back of this book. Just tear them out and put them various places, such as on your desk, car dashboard, kitchen counter, bathroom counter, dresser or television.

The more you use focal points, the more they'll become a part of you. And, the more they become a part of you, the more success you'll have in using them. God's principle of "tassels" is as valid for us today as it was in the days of early Israel. **They work!** So, give them a try, and I think you'll be encouraged to see how much they help you remember to do things God's way throughout the day.

FOR INDEPENDENT AND GROUP STUDY

1. Approximately how much of the time do you think your attitudes, thoughts and actions are pleasing to God? 90%, 50%, 10% or less?

2. Explain the principle for focal points (Numbers 15:37-41).

3. What are three specific areas of your life in which you think focal points can help you be more Christ-like (i.e. driving in traffic, communicating with your mate or children, working on your job, etc.)?

4. How does your willpower relate to the effectiveness of focal points?

5. Which of the focal points printed on the tear-out sheets in the back of this book do you think will help you the most, and why?

"AND MY GOD SHALL SUPPLY ALL YOUR NEEDS ACCORDING TO HIS RICHES IN GLORY IN CHRIST JESUS."

Philippians 4:19

CHAPTER TEN

VISUALIZING YOUR REAL AUDIENCE

As I pulled into our driveway one afternoon, I stopped abruptly. "I can't believe it!" I thought to myself. "She left her bicycle in the middle of the driveway again!" I was referring to my five year old daughter's bicycle, and I couldn't help but steam inside when I thought of how many times I had asked her not to leave her bicycle in the driveway. And, there it was again! My first inclination was to rush into the house, scold her for a few minutes, and then tell her to put the bicycle away. But, instead of giving into my natural reaction, I practiced a principle God has given us from His word.

> "**Whatever you do,** do your work heartily, **as for the Lord** rather than for man; knowing that from the Lord you will receive the reward of the inheritance. It is the Lord Christ whom you serve."
>
> Colossians 3:23-24

"Whatever you do" means just what it says. It includes **everything we do!** "As for the Lord" means the one we really should be doing things for is Jesus Christ. We shouldn't be doing things just to please ourselves or anyone else, but Him. Paul explained that principle even further when he wrote, "It is the Lord Christ whom you serve." Instead of giving in to my anger because the bicycle was in my way, **I pictured Jesus sitting in the car next to me.** I've found that to be an effective way to determine how He would handle a situation. Well, I was sure He wouldn't have gone into the house ranting and raving as I felt like doing. Just picturing Jesus sitting next to me immediately gave me a different perspective of the situation. All of a sudden I saw it as just an act of my little girl's forgetfulness rather than a case of disobedience that should be tried by the Supreme Court. "Why don't you move the bicycle?" I imagined Jesus asking me. I immediately got out of the car and put the bicycle away with the peaceful attitude I was doing it for my Lord. Of course, I still had my responsibility to call it to my daughter's attention when I got into the house as something she needed to keep working on.

I've carried this practice of visualizing Jesus sitting or standing next to me into many types of situations I face throughout the day. And, it's amazing how much more willing I am to do things I would have balked at when I picture Him personally asking me to do them. Try it the next time someone asks you to do something that's neither easy nor convenient to do. We all have opportunities to practice this type of visualizing, don't we? Perhaps we'll imagine Him asking us to take the garbage out, or clean up someone else's mess, or give someone a ride into town.

The next time you're in one of these kinds of situations, try visualizing Jesus personally asking you to get it done. **And, what you'll be picturing in your mind is a reality!** Most likely Jesus would personally ask you to do it if He was physically present, unless He'd beat you to it! Remember, it was Jesus, Himself, who got down on His knees to wash His disciples' dirty feet. It sure gives you more enthusiasm when you know you're really doing something because He personally has asked you to do it. **It's Jesus Christ whom you serve!**

FOR INDEPENDENT AND GROUP STUDY

1. From one of your own experiences, tell how visualizing Jesus next to you would have helped you deal with that situation better.

2. How can visualizing the presence of Jesus help you carry out the action of 2 Corinthians 10:5?

PART THREE

GETTING TO KNOW JESUS BETTER

AN INTRODUCTION TO THE NEXT 15 CHAPTERS

Now that you know some of what's involved in becoming Christ-like, let's get started in getting to know Him better. Jesus Christ's teaching ministry covered over a three year period. And, in that time, through His words and actions, He gave us a pattern for conducting our lives. In the next 15 chapters, we'll look at episodes from His life to help us learn from Him how He wants us to conduct ourselves, as we're empowered by the Holy Spirit. Of course, these chapters are only bite-sized looks into the life of Jesus. But, they're a start in helping us better know what He'd do in our situations.

You'll find it most beneficial to read the full account of each episode from your Bible to capture it's full flavor before you actually read it in one of the following chapters. Then, you'll have a better foundation upon which you can apply the principles from His life. The following is an explanation of how to effectively use the format of the next 15 chapters to relate Jesus' life to your daily situations.

JESUS IN ACTION. It's in this section you'll read about an episode from Jesus' life. As you read about what He said and did, it's my hope that you'll get a more indepth look at Jesus and come to know Him more intimately.

PERSONAL APPLICATION. Knowing what Jesus did in His situations is different from knowing what He'd do in ours. So, in this section, we'll relate His words and actions to where we live today.

FOCAL POINT. The focal point in each chapter is a word or sentence describing **a type** of situation we face, just as Jesus did.

POSSIBLE IDENTIFIERS. An "identifier" is a specific situation of yours which can relate to the focal point. Two or three sample identifiers are given in each chapter with additional spaces for you to fill in some of your own.

Well, it's time to get started to explore the life of the most amazing Man who ever lived. The only Man who claimed to be God **and backed it up with His words and actions.** When you're following Jesus Christ, you're following God. When you're becoming Christ-like in your situations, you're being maximized to the potential God has intended for you. **And, as you begin to carry out your Christ-like response in every situation, you can tell the Lord, "This is my expression of love for You!"**

CHAPTER ELEVEN

LOOKING FOR WHAT BENEFITS OTHERS
Based on John 4:1-7

JESUS IN ACTION

It was high noon when Jesus and His small band of men arrived at Jacob's Well outside of a Samaritan village. They had been walking on the dusty roads for several hours already in the hot sun. And, now they were tired and hungry. His men went into the nearby village to buy food, but Jesus decided to stay behind and rest at the well. Most likely Jesus was exhausted, not only from the walk, but from talking to His men along the way. Sitting against the well, He could see a woman approaching carrying a water jug. As she drew closer, possibly her dress, or perhaps her mannerisms, revealed she was an immoral woman. Then, too, it wasn't customary for any of the townspeople to come to the well in the heat of the day to draw water. The women usually would come in the cool of the evening when they'd draw water and share news of the day with each other. For whatever reason this woman had for coming in the heat of the day, there she was!

As Jesus watched her draw from the well, He discerned she had a problem far greater than her need for water. And, He initiated a conversation aimed at helping her meet that need. **Now, Jesus was tired and needed rest, but instead of looking out for His own interests, He looked for a way He could help benefit the woman.**

PERSONAL APPLICATION

For most of us, it's natural to want to meet our own needs before we help someone else, isn't it? Jesus must have desired that, too. Surely He was all "talked out" from His conversations with His disciples as they walked along in the hot sun. He deserved to rest. But, He gave up meeting His own need in order to help meet the woman's need. He was looking out for her benefit, rather than His own.

That isn't our natural tendency, is it? If a child begins asking us questions, and we're intent on our own project, most of us would tell the child to run along because we have serious work to do. But, to that child, the questions he wanted to ask are the most important questions in the entire world that could be asked. Or, just when we're hurrying along trying to keep on our schedule, we get another phone call. Sure, this person has needs, but so do we in order to get our work done on time. It's far easier to concentrate on satisfying our own needs than it is to help someone else, isn't it? **And, sometimes meeting our own needs will have a priority from God's perspective as well. But usually we're just caught up in doing what we want to do without considering God's perspective.**

When Jesus came down from heaven, He gave up His right to live on earth as God. He lived here as a human being, as one who had to depend on His Father in all things. Because of His total dependence on His Father, He was never out for what only benefited Himself. His only desire was to do those things pleasing to His Father. And, as ambassadors for Jesus Christ we have a responsibility to represent Him in everything we do. **And, that responsibility means helping other people meet their needs when the occasion arises.** It might even mean answering a child's quesions or talking on the phone in the midst of an already busy schedule.

Focal Point

Person in need.

Christ-Like Response

Whenever possible, look for ways you can help meet other people's needs, rather than try to meet your own needs first.

Possible Identifiers

1. A child asking questions, or trying to play with you, when you're busy with your own projects.

2. A phone call from a person with problems when you have a busy schedule to keep.

3.

4.

5.

6.

"BUT SEEK FIRST HIS KINGDOM AND HIS RIGHTEOUSNESS; AND ALL THESE THINGS SHALL BE ADDED TO YOU."

Matthew 6:33

CHAPTER TWELVE

GIVING UP YOUR RIGHT TO BE APPRECIATED

Based on John 4:1-42

JESUS IN ACTION

It was in the heat of the day, and Jesus was still talking to the immoral woman at the well. Or, at least He was trying to talk to her. Throughout their conversation she was unfriendly, evasive and outright rude. Jesus didn't have to stand for that. He could have said, "All right, if you don't want to talk, it's fine with Me!" And, then He at least could have gotten some well-deserved rest. After all, He and His men had already walked a long way in the hot sun! But, Jesus didn't give up. **He didn't want her appreciation.** He wanted to help her clean up her life! And, that could only be done if she knew who He was, and how to come into His Father's family. Well, His efforts finally paid off. Not only did this woman come to believe in Him as the Messiah, but so did many of her townspeople! **All because Jesus was more interested in helping her, than be appreciated by her!**

PERSONAL APPLICATION

Don't we all like to be appreciated? Sure, we do. It's only natural. When you work hard at making a living, or when you prepare your family's meals day after day, it's great to have someone say, "Thanks, I really appreciate you!" But, it doesn't happen as much as we'd like, does it?

It's especially good to hear those words when you go out of your way to help someone, like Jesus did. But we can better understand what real giving is by how Jesus talked to this ungrateful woman. He wasn't interested in her acknowledging His help, only in helping her. That's real unselfishness. **Not only did He give up His right to rest, but His right to be appreciated as well.** And, that's something to keep in mind as you concentrate on representing Him by helping others. Don't look for any paybacks, or even simple appreciation. Just keep on trying to help. That's Christ-likeness!

Focal Point

Person you're helping doesn't show any appreciation.

Christ-Like Response

Since real giving doesn't look for paybacks, don't expect to be appreciated. Just keep on looking for ways to help.

Possible Identifiers

1. Family members who take your help for granted.

2. Anyone who doesn't verbally, or outwardly, show appreciation for your efforts to help.

3. Someone who seems to expect you to help.

4.

5.

6.

"LET YOUR LIGHT SHINE BEFORE MEN IN SUCH A WAY THAT THEY MAY SEE YOUR GOOD WORKS, AND GLORIFY YOUR FATHER WHO IS IN HEAVEN."

Matthew 5:16

"THEREFORE YOU ARE TO BE PERFECT, AS YOUR HEAVENLY FATHER IS PERFECT."

Matthew 5:48

CHAPTER THIRTEEN

HOW TO MEET A NEW DAY

Based on Mark 1:35-38

JESUS IN ACTION

From His two-day visit in that Samaritan town, Jesus and His few men moved northward. He moved on to Cana where during a short stay, He healed a dying boy. Then He went on to Nazareth, His hometown. You'd think He would have been warmly received there, but when He claimed to be the Messiah in the Synagogue one day, the people ran Him out of town.

As He went on to Capernaum He found great popularity. His reputation for healing people had begun to go ahead of Him. Many sick people gathered around the house where Jesus was staying in Capernaum, and, out of compassion, He healed them all.

When the last "Good night" was said that evening, it was a tired Jesus who layed down for sleep. But, before daybreak He was already up walking outside to a secluded place where He could be alone with His Father in prayer. It was a new day, and Jesus, who was perhaps more tired than the rest of His men at the end of the previous day, was up before them and off to be alone with His Father.

Have you ever wondered why Jesus prayed so much? You'd think, being God, He wouldn't have had to, wouldn't you? Well, the apostle Paul helps us understand why in his letter to the Philippians.

> "...although He existed in the form of God, did not regard equality with God a thing to be

grasped, **but emptied Himself, taking the form of a bond-servant, and being made in the likeness of men.** And being found in appearance as a man, He humbled Himself by becoming obedient to the point of death, even death on a cross."

Philippians 2:6-7

We don't know what Jesus talked to His Father about in those quiet moments before daybreak. But, we have good insight from Paul why Jesus was there praying. Before He came to earth, Jesus willfully let go of all of His divine attributes. **Instead of living on earth as an equal with his Father, Jesus chose to become a bond-servant to Him. That's the only way He could really be an example to us in living God's way. And, that's why Jesus needed to pray so much.** You see, prayer helped Him maintain His mental and spiritual union with His Father, just like it does for us. Also, prayer helped Jesus discern what His priorities should be, as we'll see in our next episode of His life.

PERSONAL APPLICATION

When do you pray the most? Is it when you're the most busy or the least busy? Is it when things are good for you or when they're bad? It's easier to pray when things aren't quite so busy, or when they're bad, isn't it? Well times were the busiest for Jesus. Huge crowds of people kept coming to Him to be healed, and to hear His words. And, times were good for Him. His popularity was steadily increasing as He healed people and cast out demons. He would have been welcomed anywhere in the town of Capernaum. But in spite of how busy Jesus was, and how well things were going for Him, He consistently went to His Father in prayer.

One aspect of being Christ-like is to meet God in a secluded place each day. Why a secluded place? Well, the fewer distractions you have, the more you'll be able to focus only on God. Your secluded place might be part of your own house where no one else is. It might even have to be your bathroom! Maybe in your home a secluded place can only be found by getting up in the early morning hours before anyone else. Or, possibly your selected place will have to be a restaurant where you'll see no one who knows you, or a bench, or a parked car.

Wherever it is, go there as you start each day, and talk to God in prayer. Tell Him of your successes, failures, and your hopes and aspirations. Tell Him of your concerns for the day. Then, let Him talk to you through His word, the Bible. One way of doing this is by reading a portion out of the Bible, perhaps in the Sermon on the Mount (Matthew 5-7) and question each verse with, "What does this tell me about what I need to do?" By having something specific in mind you'll face during the day, you'll be more apt to get God's specific views on it. Getting God's perspective is one way to remain enthusiastic about serving Him even in the routine things of your job, your school, or your home. You'll find spending those moments alone with God in prayer to be the most important thing you do as you meet each new day!

Focal Point

New day.

Christ-Like Response

As each day begins, go to a secluded place to talk to God about your desires, concerns and priorities for the day. Then, let Him talk to you through His word, the Bible.

Possible Identifiers

New day.

"BEWARE OF PRACTICING YOUR RIGHTEOUSNESS BEFORE MEN TO BE NOTICED BY THEM; OTHERWISE YOU HAVE NO REWARD WITH YOUR FATHER WHO IS IN HEAVEN."

Matthew 6:1

CHAPTER FOURTEEN

SAFEGUARDING PRIORITIES

Based on Mark 1:35-39 and Luke 10:38-42

JESUS IN ACTION

Jesus was in His secluded place praying that early morning when He heard footsteps approaching. Peter and the rest of Jesus' disciples came looking for Him, and when they finally found Him they excitedly shouted, "Everyone is looking for You." Apparently, because of the excitement of so many healings the night before, news spread throughout the town and more people had come to the house where Jesus was staying. What an opportunity Jesus had to shower God's love on them by healing their sick bodies. And, what a surprise it must have been to His disciples when Jesus replied, "Let's go on to the other towns in order that I might preach there also, for that's the reason I came out."

Now, where was His enthusiasm for healing people? Why didn't Jesus stay in Capernaum where He was obviously needed and popular? The people wanted Him to stay so badly. Oh, it would have been very easy for Him to be caught up in the wave of popularity He was experiencing. And, He probably could have increased it even more by staying in Capernaum. But, Jesus had His priorities in order. **His real mission was to bring people the good news of how to come into God's family, and healings were only a secondary purpose.**

We also see Jesus keeping His right priority in another situation, and on another day. It was when He was visiting the house of Mary and Martha. Martha was working hard at preparing a meal for her guest. But her sister, Mary, was content in letting Martha do all of the work while she sat by Jesus listening to His every word. There was Martha busily preparing the meal with all the trimmings, and there was Mary talking with Jesus.

"It just doesn't seem fair!" Martha must have thought to herself. "I'm doing all of the work and she just sits there!" Finally, she couldn't restrain herself any longer. She went over to Jesus and asked Him to tell Mary to come and help her. **But, again we see Jesus sizing up priorities as they related to His overall purpose.** "Martha, Martha," He replied, "you're **worried** and bothered about so many things..." And, that's exactly what Martha was. This particular Greek word for "worried" has been used to describe someone who is seeking to promote their own interests. Perhaps that's how Jesus meant it here. You see, Jesus knew Martha was going beyond what was really necessary to prepare that meal. She didn't have to make such an elaborate setting. Only one dish of food was really necessary to satisfy their hunger. But apparently Martha had many extras. And, because of the word Jesus used to describe her, we can assume these extras were more designed to give her recognition as a warm hostess than to meet the hunger of her guest. Her focus was on herself rather than on Jesus. And, that's what Jesus was pointing out. He sized up the activities of each sister as to what He thought was most important. And, taking in God's word, which Mary was doing, was more important than preparing an elaborate meal, which Martha was doing.

"Only a few things are necessary," Jesus told Martha. "Really only one, for Mary has chosen the good part, which cannot be taken away from her." Yes, the meal was necessary, but if Martha had been seeing things from Jesus' perspective, she would have prepared a simple meal and then sat back and enjoyed fellowship with Him. In the same way, many weeks earlier, healing people in Capernaum was a good thing, but going on to other towns to present the good news was the **best** thing to do.

PERSONAL APPLICATION

Choosing the best in the midst of many good things is difficult to do. And, we frequently make the wrong choices. Jesus was capable of making the wrong choices, too. Let's remember, He emptied Himself of His divine attributes in order to live on earth in human form as a total bond-servant to His Father. He left equality with His Father behind in order to take on a servant's role to Him.

As He discussed His concerns for each day in prayer with His Father, His Father gave Him the right perspective on what things had priorities over others. So, that's the first thing we need to keep in mind in safeguarding our priorities. Make sure you talk to God in large segments of time as well as on the spur of the moment. **Talk to Him about what you consider to be important and ask Him to show you, from His word, what's important from His perspective. Ask yourself what choice Jesus would make if He was standing in your place. What would Jesus consider the "good" thing and what would He consider the "best" thing?**

Let's take a look at some of the more common things over which we have trouble establishing priorities. First, what do you think Jesus would choose for you between spending several hours a week watching television as over against spending the same hours talking, playing games, reading and relating with your family? Secondly, what would Jesus choose for you between spending many hours preparing a seven-course dinner for guests and preparing something more informal where you'll be more relaxed and have time to talk and get better acquainted? Thirdly, what would Jesus choose for you between finishing up a project which could cause you to be late for an appointment and being there on time?

I don't think we need to go any further, do we? Our problem is the same as Martha's. **Often we're caught up in our own desires, without our focus on Jesus, so it's difficult to choose the best over the good.** That's why beginning each day in prayer is so important. Then, as you go through each day, keep in mind your greatest responsibility is to be Jesus Christ's personal ambassador. When you see yourself that way, it'll be much easier to choose the best over the good.

Focal Point

A need to know what to do.

Christ-Like Response

Evaluate what you're doing as to what has the highest priority for that moment from God's perspective.

Possible Identifiers

1. Worktime versus leisuretime.
2. Familytime versus television.
3.
4.
5.
6.

"AND WHEN YOU ARE PRAYING, DO NOT USE MEANINGLESS REPETITION, AS THE GENTILES DO, FOR THEY SUPPOSE THAT THEY WILL BE HEARD FOR THEIR MANY WORDS."

Matthew 6:7

"THEREFORE DO NOT BE ANXIOUS FOR TOMORROW; FOR TOMORROW WILL CARE FOR ITSELF. EACH DAY HAS ENOUGH TROUBLE OF ITS OWN."

Matthew 6:34

CHAPTER FIFTEEN

TAKE A MOMENT TO BE MORE EFFECTIVE

Based on Luke 5:1-3

JESUS IN ACTION

Excitement swarmed around Jesus as He walked along the shore of the Lake of Gennesaret. He was followed by a huge crowd of enthusiastic people. They continued to press around Him which made it hard for Him to teach them what was on His mind. They had never heard anyone speak with such great authority who still seemed to understand them so well. Perhaps some of the people were trying to push their way next to Him just to ask a question, or just to touch Him so their bodies would be healed. For whatever reasons, their enthusiasm was making it extra hard for Jesus to get His message across. And He found it necessary to pause and consider a more effective way of getting the job done. Looking around, He saw Simon Peter's fishing boat by the shore. So, He got in and asked Peter to push the boat out a short distance from shore. Then, from His new vantage point, Jesus began to teach the waiting crowd in a far more effective way.

PERSONAL APPLICATION

Sometimes circumstances push in on us just like they did on Jesus. And, it's easy to be overwhelmed by them. We need to look for possible solutions to make us more effective in the things we do just as Jesus did. He could have put up with His circumstances and tried to talk louder. Or, He could have circulated among the different groups of people so they all could hear parts of what He was saying. **But, He chose to take time to consider how He could be the most effective.** So, looking around, He came up with an answer. And, in that brief moment, He saw a boat that would help Him get the job done more effectively.

For whatever time you have before having to take action, or even in the middle of doing something, try sizing up your situation for what you can do to maximize your efforts. **Remember, being at your maximum effectiveness is part of representing Jesus Christ.** Perhaps, as you clean up the house, it means listening to Christian music to keep your mind on the "things above rather than the things on earth," and the dust on the tables. Or, perhaps it means making better use of your time as you drive to and from work by listening to teachings from God's word on cassette tapes. Or, perhaps it means asking for help to get your many responsibilities done when you have a pressing deadline. **You'll find you'll become more effective at what you do when you bother to take a few minutes to think of how to do it more effectively. And, that's part of being Christ-like.**

Focal Point

Working on a project.

Christ-Like Response

Take a moment to determine how you can be the most effective in getting your job done.

Possible Identifiers

1. Cleaning the house.

2. Rushing towards a deadline.

3.

4.

5.

6.

"THEREFORE EVERY ONE WHO HEARS THESE WORDS OF MINE, AND ACTS UPON THEM, MAY BE COMPARED TO A WISE MAN, WHO BUILT HIS HOUSE UPON THE ROCK."

Matthew 7:24

"THESE THINGS I HAVE SPOKEN TO YOU, THAT IN ME YOU MAY HAVE PEACE. IN THE WORLD YOU HAVE TRIBULATION, BUT TAKE COURAGE; I HAVE OVERCOME THE WORLD."

John 16:33

CHAPTER SIXTEEN

SHOW NO PARTIALITY
Based on Luke 5:12-13

JESUS IN ACTION

Jesus had been moving on from town to town with his men, bringing His message of salvation to all who would listen. Wherever He went He created excitement. He spoke with authority, not like many of the so-called religious authorities of the day. When He spoke, people listened. And, they came! In one of these towns a man full of the dreaded disease, leprosy, must have seen Jesus talking to the townspeople. Then, when Jesus was off by Himself he rushed up to Him and fell on his face before Him. I imagine Jesus' disciples must have been thinking it was a good thing the man wasn't showing his face. For leprosy was the type of disease that would eat away a person's flesh and make him look hideous. The man begged Jesus, saying, "Lord, if You're willing, You can make me clean." He knew Jesus could heal him. But he wasn't sure if Jesus had the stomach for it!

How thrilled that leper must have been when Jesus said, "I am willing," and stretched out His hand and actually touched him! I can just see the eyes of His disciples practically popping out. A man actually touching a leper! Not only did people refuse to touch lepers, but they ran the other way when one was coming shouting, "Unclean! Unclean!" But Jesus didn't. He healed the rich, the poor, the outcasts, the merchants, the young and the old alike. And, even a leper! **Jesus showed no partiality.**

Let's note Jesus didn't choose to heal this man at a distance, although He had healed other people at a distance when the need arose. But, He chose to demonstrate His compassion for this "undesirable" person with His own **personal touch.** And that, by the way, was a beginning of widespread popularity for Jesus. Up until that time He could easily go into a city and only a few people recognized Him. But now, He couldn't go into a city, after healing that leper, without being mobbed by people showing their enthusiasm for this man who not only spoke with authority but loved everyone of them.

PERSONAL APPLICATION

Many people find it difficult to pay personal attention to someone who isn't accepted by normal standards. Perhaps he lacks social graces, or has the wrong color of skin, or the wrong beliefs, or doesn't have an accepted amount of education. Or, perhaps he's just painfully egotistical and unpleasant to be around. Sure, it would be easy to avoid such people. And we normally do. Jesus could have avoided the leper, but He didn't! He saw within this person a specially designed individual with an unfortunate problem. And, He got personally involved with him, rather than try to avoid him.

It's a lot easier just to associate with people with whom you have things in common, isn't it? But Jesus was a man for all the people. The rich and the beggars, the educated and the uneducated, the people in powerful positions and those you forget the name of as soon as you're introduced. He was often criticized because He associated with the outcasts. But, Jesus didn't show partiality. **Each person was uniquely designed and had feelings.** Each person had the capacity to love or to hate. Each person had the capacity to cry or to laugh! Each person was an individual! And Jesus associated with them. As a personal ambassador for Jesus Christ to each person you meet, you have an opportunity to reach out His arms to that person, regardless of his outward appearance. All most people need is someone who believes in them and cares enough to get involved, without showing partiality.

Focal Point

"Undesirable" person

Christ-Like Response

See him as a uniquely designed individual. Then, personally involve yourself to help him blossom into the person God intends him to become.

Possible Identifiers

1. Person no one seems to like.

2. Person, either more educated, or less educated, than you.

3.

4.

5.

6.

"IF YOU WERE OF THE WORLD, THE WORLD WOULD LOVE ITS OWN; BUT BECAUSE YOU ARE NOT OF THE WORLD, BUT I CHOSE YOU OUT OF THE WORLD, THEREFORE THE WORLD HATES YOU."

John 15:19

CHAPTER SEVENTEEN

SEEING SOMEONE'S POTENTIAL

Based on Luke 5:27-28

JESUS IN ACTION

Jesus had just amazed a house full of people by healing a paralyzed man. Now, as He was walking along the beach, many people were following Him and listening to His every word. Off in the distance was a tax collector's stand. And, in those days tax collectors were liked about as well as the measles. They weren't! Tax collectors were considered traitors because they were Jews who worked for the Roman government, collecting money from their own Jewish people. And, many of them lined their own pockets by charging more than what was required. Calling someone a "tax collector" was one of the foulest forms of insult.

If you had been in the crowd following Jesus that day, what would you have thought as He stopped in front of Levi's tax stand? You might have hoped He was going to scold Levi for his underhanded methods. What a surprise it was for many of those onlookers when Jesus invited Levi to become one of His followers! While others looked at Levi and saw a crook, Jesus looked at him and saw his potential of becoming one of His followers. While others looked at Levi and saw a traitor to his own people, Jesus looked at him and saw a man who would become totally committed to Him. **And, because of the faith Jesus had in Levi, we know him today as Matthew, author of the first Gospel of Jesus Christ!**

PERSONAL APPLICATION

There's a good possibility many of us would have written off someone like Levi after first meeting him, isn't there? We might have thought, "He's not my type." Or, "What will others think of me if I accept such a man as a friend?" Levi didn't fit the mold of what some might consider to be proper Christian company. And, even in the world's eyes he was a type of an outcast. **We usually size up people from our own standards of what we consider important, don't we?** Are they attractive? What's their financial status? What are their talents? How do they make a living? How can they help me? Jesus also sized up people from the standard He considered to be important. But, His only standard was, "How willing is the person to follow Me?" That is how He sized up Levi.

You can be Christ-like in dealing with people by looking for the real person behind the many masks he or she might be wearing. Perhaps they aren't a follower of Jesus at the present time, but could they possibly show an interest if they had the opportunity? Do what you can to cultivate that interest. Perhaps your best way would be to give that person a direct invitation to follow Jesus, just as Jesus gave Levi. Or, it might be a casual conversation through which you can communicate to him how Jesus affects your life.

But, keep in mind an outward appearance isn't always the best indicator of how the person will respond to Jesus. **Try looking through their present circumstances to their potential for change once they commit themselves to follow Jesus as a way of life.** Jesus saw in Levi what he could become, rather than what he was at the present time. Someday, when Jesus returns for us, each Christian actually will be conformed to His likeness because we'll be in His very presence (1 John 3:2)!

Focal Point

Everybody with whom you have contact.

Christ-Like Response

Look beyond their outward appearance to the real person they can become in Jesus Christ.

Possible Identifiers

1. Your child who has gotten into mischief again.
2. The loud person who people can't stand.
3.
4.
5.
6.

"GREATER LOVE HAS NO ONE THAN THIS, THAT ONE LAY DOWN HIS LIFE FOR HIS FRIENDS. YOU ARE MY FRIENDS, IF YOU DO WHAT I COMMAND YOU."

John 15:13-14

CHAPTER EIGHTEEN

HANDLING PRESSURE ON YOUR CONVICTIONS
Based on Luke 6:6-11

JESUS IN ACTION

Jesus was now just entering into His second full year of ministry, following a very eventful first year. He had already rid the profiteers from the temple for the first time, and had His historic "born again" conversation with Nicodemus, a leading Pharisee. Then, on His way to the northern territory He had His well known talk with the woman at the well. Although He was run out of His own hometown, Nazareth, He was gaining in popularity among the people elsewhere. The close of His first year's ministry was climaxed by Jesus healing a leper, shocking the Pharisees by forgiving a paralytic of his sins, as well as healing him, and asking a hated tax collector to be one of His followers.

Now, as He moved into His second full year of ministry, He began to experience increasing opposition from the religious leaders. Jesus had certainly become a force to be reckoned with in teaching about God's ways. The religious leaders felt that, if He would be allowed to continue on like this, most of the people would believe in Him and the Romans would come and take away their nation (John 11:48). **So, they tried to do anything they could to find fault in Him because they wanted to turn the people against Him.**

It was on such an occasion when Jesus was teaching on the Sabbath in a local synagogue. Pharisees were mixed in with the crowd, that day, listening intently to His every word, hoping He would make one mistake. Jesus knew that.

Then, He noticed a man with a badly withered hand. Most likely many of the other people had seen the man, felt sorry for him, but couldn't do anything for Him. Jesus could do something. He knew it was against the tradition of the Pharisees to heal on the Sabbath, and He knew they were waiting to accuse Him of breaking one of those traditions. In full knowledge of this, Jesus told the man with the withered hand to come forward. Boldly Jesus asked the crowd, "Is it lawful on the Sabbath to do good, or to do evil, to save a life or to destroy it?" Then, Jesus asked the man to stretch out his hand, and as many witnesses watched, the man's hand was completely restored. The religious leaders were enraged by Jesus' action. He dared to defy them, and their way of doing things, in the presence of many people! From that time on, the Pharisees discussed together how they could stop this man who openly defied them and their traditions.

PERSONAL APPLICATION

Following Jesus is one thing. But, it's still another to have to buck the way things are ordinarily done when pressure is on you to conform, isn't it? For instance, as a follower of Jesus, how do you handle your convictions as a result of off-color humor at the office or at school? The traditional and accepted way to handle it is to join right in and even tell a few yourself. Do you stay around and listen so you can be accepted by those who enjoy such off-color humor? How do you handle your convictions when you hear gossip about other people? Do you listen interestedly and even add a few bits of your own information? Or, do you try to point out the best qualities of the person, and even try to change the subject? How do you handle your personal convictions at social gatherings? Do you do everything everyone else does because it's expected of you? Or, do you do what Jesus would do regardless of what others will say or think?

Abiding by our convictions is pretty hard to do, isn't it? We want to be accepted by other people and be considered a "regular" person. Well, Jesus often faced pressure from authoritative people regarding His convictions. The Pharisees constantly tried to pressure Him into their tiny world of distorted values. But, Jesus was true to His convictions because He was committed to do things only to please His Father, not Himself. And, when Jesus stood in front of that crowd in the synagogue, beside a man with a withered hand, He knew what His convictions called Him to do. And, that was to heal the man's hand rather than be pressurized by what tradition said shouldn't be done on the Sabbath.

Focal Point

Your convictions are challenged or pressured.

Christ-Like Response

Hold true to your Christ-like convictions, regardless of what others will say or think, because your only responsibility is to be an ambassador for Jesus Christ. And, you're totally accepted by Him!

Possible Identifiers

1. When something you believe in is challenged.

2. When you hear gossip about someone.

3.

4.

5.

6.

"I AM THE VINE, YOU ARE THE BRANCHES; HE WHO ABIDES IN ME, AND I IN HIM, HE BEARS MUCH FRUIT; FOR APART FROM ME YOU CAN DO NOTHING."

John 15:5

CHAPTER NINETEEN

HAVING EMPATHY
Based on John 11:17-37

JESUS IN ACTION

The countdown to Jesus' crucifixion had started. He was pressing onward to Jerusalem where He would experience His own painful death. On His way, Jesus and His men received news their good friend Lazarus was extremely sick. But instead of hurrying to Lazarus' side, Jesus remained where He was for two days longer. He knew He must wait in order for His Father's purpose to be fulfilled. When Jesus and His men finally arrived in Bethany, Lazarus had already been in the tomb for four days. His sisters, Mary and Martha, were at home being comforted by many of the Jewish people from nearby Jerusalem. Someone must have seen Jesus come into town because Martha soon received word He had arrived. She immediately ran out to meet Him. "Lord, if You had been here my brother would not have died," she said. "But I know that even now, God will give you whatever you ask."

Although Martha was grieved for her brother, she was also calm and rational. It's possible she found new strength in just having Jesus present. When Jesus told her Lazarus would rise again, she was able to reply that she knew he would on the last day. She was able to carry on a conversation that was factual and full of information concerning the resurrection from the dead. And, Jesus met her where she was, and talked with her.

But when she came back to tell her sister that Jesus had arrived, we see another picture. Mary rushed out of the house in a bundle of emotions. She raced to Jesus and fell at His feet. "Lord, if you had been here my brother would not have died," Mary sobbed. She knew Jesus could have healed her brother if He had been there on time. Perhaps she was blaming Him. Whatever was on her mind, she was very emotional. And, Jesus took that into consideration. He didn't have many words for Mary. She wasn't interested in discussing facts about the resurrection, and Jesus knew it. He simply asked, "Where have you laid him?" Then, He, too, broke into tears. He met Mary on her emotional level just as He had met Martha on her emotional level. What a graphic display of empathy Jesus had for both Mary and Martha.

PERSONAL APPLICATION

Empathy is the capacity to participate in someone else's feelings. Jesus had empathy for both women. He was sincere in His comments to Martha, and the tears that streamed from His eyes, when He saw Mary, were also genuine. You see, Jesus had total empathy for everyone with whom He encountered. That's hard for us to do, isn't it? Often when we see a weakness in another person, we judge. Instead of getting inside that person and trying to understand their weakness, we condemn them for having it. Especially if it's an area we ourselves don't have under control.

We frequently fail to feel with other people. All we want to do is be logical and help that person understand everything is going to be alright. Like when a small child comes to us with a slightly hurt finger. For some of us, it's natural to say, "Oh, that's alright. It really doesn't hurt that much, does it?" But those words don't empathize with the hurt or fear inside the child. Yes, the child needs assurance it'll be alright as you give his hurt immediate attention. But, the child also needs his emotional needs cared for. You're empathizing when you hold the child close in your arms, and let him know you understand his fear and upsetness.

Or, when your wife is panicking to get the house in order for company, right then she doesn't need to hear, "Oh, come on! They live in a house too, ya know. They know what it's like to keep things in order. They'll understand." To enter into her feelings is to understand that to her it's important things be tidied up before they arrive. Empathy says, "I know you've had so much to do today." Empathy gives her your pair of hands to help get things cleaned up in time.

Or, when your husband is feeling the pressure from completing a project on time. He doesn't need to hear, "Well, you shouldn't have played tennis the other day," or "Don't worry honey, you'll get it done." Empathy enters into his feelings by listening and asking what you can do to help. Empathy is your hands massaging his shoulders, and perhaps you saying that together you can work things out. You see, empathy isn't the natural way to go, but it is the way Jesus went. And that, my friend, is a Christ-like quality.

Focal Point

A person showing an emotional, spiritual or physical need.

Christ-Like Response

Try to mentally and emotionally look inside the person to see how they feel. Try to see things from their perspective. Then, in words, or action, let them know you understand.

Possible Identifiers

1. Someone complaining.

2. Someone emotionally upset.

3. Someone physically exhausted.

4.

5.

6.

"YOU ARE THE LIGHT OF THE WORLD. A CITY SET ON A HILL CANNOT BE HIDDEN."

Matthew 5:14

CHAPTER TWENTY

NO ODDS AGAINST GOD'S RESULTS

Based on John 11:34-44

JESUS IN ACTION

After Jesus initially comforted Mary and Martha in their grief over their brother's death, He asked where Lazarus had been buried. The sisters led the way to the tomb as Jesus followed closely behind, along with His men and many people who had come to comfort Mary and Martha. Lazarus had been dead for four days and his body was already in the state of decomposition. **The human odds were definitely against Lazarus coming back to life.** After all, it's not possible for a decaying body to become whole again! Not even with all the aids of modern science. No one could have possibly known what a great thing was about to happen. No one, but Jesus! Let's remember, Jesus didn't go by human odds.

When He commanded the stone to be moved away, Martha said, "Lord, by this time there will be a stench; for he has been dead for four days." But He insisted, and they moved away the stone. What a scene that must have been. Many of the onlookers probably wondered why He wanted the stone rolled away. His own disciples quite possibly thought He was carrying things just a bit too far. And, there was Martha, embarrassed about the possibility of everyone getting exposed to the stench. Jesus turned to the two sisters and said, "Did I not say to you, if you believe, you will see the glory of God?" Then He raised His eyes towards the skies and prayed to His Father. He told His Father He was praying aloud because He wanted all the people to know it really was God the Father who sent Jesus to earth. Then, in a dramatic moment, Jesus shouted, "Lazarus, come forth!" And, Lazarus did come forth. No longer a decomposing dead body. He hopped to the tomb entrance still wrapped in his burial linens. **What a thrill it must have been for Jesus' disciples and the rest of the people to see there weren't any odds against what God can do, when He wants to do it!** And, what a thrill for Mary and Martha to have their brother back again!

PERSONAL APPLICATION

It can be discouraging when you face situations with seemingly everything against you. Perhaps you're applying for a job with several others and you have the least experience. Or, perhaps you're taking an entrance exam, but had very little sleep and you feel like you're coming down with the flu. From a human perspective it doesn't look like your chances are very good in either getting the job or passing the exam. But, let's remember. There was no chance Lazarus could have come back to life either, without God causing it to happen.

Now, just knowing God can do anything He wishes won't necessarily help you get the job or pass the exam. But, it will help you, if, in discouraging situations, you keep in mind there are no odds against what God can do in carrying out His perfect plan for you. If God wants you to have that job, you'll get it experience or not. If God wants you to pass that exam, and you've prepared for it, He can help you pass it even in the face of fatigue and the flu.

When you tackle situations that look like you're defeated before you begin, keep in mind there are no odds against what God wants to bring about. But, it'll take effort on your part, just as Jesus had to walk that two days journey to get to Lazarus' tomb. God could have done it without Jesus even being there, but it wouldn't have had the impact God wanted the raising of Lazarus to have. With that in mind, you'll be able to release yourself totally towards what you're doing, in line with God's values, and trust that God will bring about the results He wants. **And, you'll be able to accept those results because you've given your best and God is in total control.**

Focal Point

Facing a difficult or discouraging situation.

Christ-Like Response

Wholeheartedly pursue your task, if it's in line with God's values, and realize God can cause the situation to work out in your favor if that's His plan. Then, accept whatever results come about, realizing that's what God chose to do.

Possible Identifiers

1. Preparing for an exam.

2. Applying for a job.

3.

4.

5.

6.

"AND WHY DO YOU LOOK AT THE SPECK IN YOUR BROTHER'S EYE, BUT DO NOT NOTICE THE LOG THAT IS IN YOUR EYE?"

Matthew 7:3

CHAPTER TWENTY-ONE

EXPOSING ANOTHER PERSON'S WEAKNESS

Based on Mark 10:17-22

JESUS IN ACTION

Jesus' fame spread like wildfire after He raised Lazarus from the dead. But, now the religious leaders were even more determined to step up their campaign to stop Him. They were afraid the Roman government would see Jesus as a threat and send troups to take away all of their remaining freedoms (John 11:48). And, Jesus knew how the religious leaders felt about Him. He knew the end was near and He was beginning to close out His teaching ministry and press forward to the cross.

As He and His men were passing through one of the many towns, a prominent man ran up to Him, fell on his knees in front of Jesus and asked, "Good teacher, what shall I do to inherit eternal life?" What a sight that must have been! Here's a respectable, wealthy and probably socially prominent man of the town on his knees in the dirt, pleading with Jesus.

And, he had a legitimate question. So, you can imagine how disappointed he was when Jesus told him about keeping all of the Old Testament commandments. "Teacher," he replied, "I've kept all these things from my youth up." Apparently this man, in his own eyes, didn't have any weaknesses. But Jesus, looking at him with love, saw there was something still lacking. And, He diplomatically and gently tried to help the man see his own weakness. "One thing you lack," Jesus told him, "Go and sell all of your possessions and give the money to the poor. And you'll have treasure in heaven. Then, come and follow Me."

Now, that really hit home. And, that's why the man was so sad. He must have realized his love for the Lord wasn't as great as his love for his own possessions. Jesus wasn't against this man's wealth in itself. He was against anything keeping this man from an all out commitment of following Him. In this man's situation, it just happened to be his wealth.

That was an interesting way to point out the man's weakness, wasn't it? Instead of clobbering him with how materialistic he was, Jesus told him something to do. But, let's notice Jesus also told him of the reward he'd have in doing it. Eternal treasure in heaven! And, then he challenged him to consider an all out commitment to follow along with Him. Because of the approach Jesus took, this man was able to see his own weakness, probably for the first time in his life. He didn't get defensive about it, just disappointed that he couldn't make that type of commitment.

PERSONAL APPLICATION

Most of us find it difficult to confront someone about a weakness, don't we? Perhaps, it's because we don't know how they'll receive our words or how they'll respond to us. Maybe it's because were afraid the confrontation will cause permanent damage to our relationship with the person. Well, let's notice again how Jesus went about it.

First, Jesus saw the man out of love. He was more interested in the man more effectively following Him, than He was in blasting him with his weakness. That's the first thing to keep in mind as you consider showing someone his weakness. Are you really doing it because you have a genuine love for the person and are interested in helping him reach his potential in following Jesus, or are you just annoyed with him?

Now, let's notice how Jesus went about showing this wealthy man his weakness. **He gave him something to do that He knew would cause the man to see his problem.** Giving his money to the poor wouldn't bring any material profit to the man. That's why Jesus quickly followed by telling him the eternal reward he'd have from God. But, the man's focus wasn't on God as much as he thought it was, so the reward wasn't that appealing to him. **Most likely this was a blind area for the man to see about himself. We all have areas like that.** We think we're more committed to our Lord than we really are.

A possible way to help show someone you know their weakness is to either ask them a question or give them something to do, as Jesus did. **But, do it with transparency.** Remember, we all have those blind areas that keep us from more effectively following Jesus. Perhaps you know someone who is consistently late, and his habit seems to be hurting his witness for the Lord. It would be a little harsh to say, "Jim, why don't you start having a little more consideration for all the people you always keep waiting?" And, Jim probably would get a little defensive, and start banging away at your weaknesses. It's fine to have someone point out your weaknesses, and you should welcome it if you really want to more effectively follow Jesus. But, more than likely his motive for doing it would be just to cover up his own weakness, and you would have defeated your very reason for confronting him.

Another more Christ-like way to approach your friend might be, "Jim, many people think that not making every effort to be on time shows disrespect for other people. If that's true, then I've got a problem. I know you really do care about other people, but I also know you're late a lot of the time. What do you think you'd have to do to make yourself on time, so you can let people know you really do care about them in that particular way?" Now, Jim might never have considered his lateness as being disrespectful to anyone. And, this might be a real eye opener for him.

Our responsibility in exposing another person to their weaknesses is to approach him the same way Jesus would if He was physically there to do it. Make sure your motive is love for the person and want to help him more effectively follow Jesus. Then, do it in a way you'll be helping him evaluate his weakness, without banging him over the head with it. **Love, gentleness, respect and diplomacy are all Christ-like qualities in helping a friend become more like Jesus Christ!**

Focal Point

Someone with a weakness that's keeping them from effectively following Jesus Christ.

Christ-Like Response

Out of your love for the person, and interest in helping him mature in Christ, ask a question or give him something to do to help him see his weakness. Then, encourage him to work on it in order to more effectively follow in the steps of Christ.

Possible Identifiers

1. Someone who gossips about others.

2. Someone who is consistently late.

3.

4.

5.

6.

"AND IF YOUR BROTHER SINS, GO AND REPROVE HIM IN PRIVATE; IF HE LISTENS TO YOU, YOU HAVE WON YOUR BROTHER."

Matthew 18:15

"GO THEREFORE AND MAKE DISCIPLES OF ALL THE NATIONS, BAPTIZING THEM IN THE NAME OF THE FATHER AND THE SON AND THE HOLY SPIRIT, TEACHING THEM TO OBSERVE ALL THAT I COMMANDED YOU; AND LO, I AM WITH YOU ALWAYS, EVEN TO THE END."

Matthew 28:18-20

CHAPTER TWENTY-TWO

CURBING YOUR ANGER
Based on John 2:14-22 and Mark 11:11-18

JESUS IN ACTION

It was a wild scene that day in the temple when coins were flying through the air, animals scurrying to get out of the way and wild-eyed merchants wondering what was going on. Who was this man throwing their money-making scheme into a shambles? None other than an angry Jesus in action! Jesus actually rid the temple from these profiteers twice. First, when He began His ministry (John 2:14-22) and in the last days of His ministry (Mark 11:11-18). **Both times He was angry and both times His Father's reputation was at stake.**

Jesus had been in the Jerusalem temple many times prior to either of these episodes occurring. He knew what was going on, and it wasn't pleasing to Him. A portion of the temple area was divided into many stalls with various livestock and fowl being sold to people who wanted to offer them as sacrifices. Many visitors came to Jerusalem without the Jewish half-shekel which was needed to pay their annual temple tax. So, money changers were on hand to convert the visitors money into the Jewish half-shekel. But these money changers were driven by the profit motive, and added a certain percentage for their own living expenses.

Just before the second episode, in the last days of Jesus' ministry, He came into the temple, looked around, and then went back to Bethany where He was staying for the night. **Jesus had a whole night to think over what He would do.** And, He didn't return to the scene the next day completely unemotional. He was intent on achieving His Father's purpose, ridding the temple of profiteers. There was a purposeful design in His actions. He didn't simply walk up to the sellers and say, "Pardon Me, but I do believe you're trying to make a profit in My Father's house. That's not right, you know. Now please pick up your things and move on to the market place." Do you think they would have done it? Of course not! Jesus knew just what authoritative actions were needed to clean up His Father's house.

He boldly walked up to the sellers and turned over their tables. He used a scourge the first time to chase out the animals. The second time He drove out the buyers and sellers with His hands. The first time He scattered the sheep and oxen. The second time He wouldn't even permit people to carry containers through the temple. Jesus was a man of action, and in full control of what He was doing!

Then, when He finished ridding the temple of those who were making a mockery of it, He taught and healed the people who were really there to worship God. Certainly we have a picture of a man with reason to be angry. And He was in full control of that anger!

PERSONAL APPLICATION

If Jesus obviously demonstrated anger when He shook up the temple profiteers, would it be wrong for us to demonstrate anger when circumstances don't go our way? **Now, you'll notice Jesus was angry because His Father's reputation was at stake.** That's not our usual reason for getting angry, is it? We get angry when our circumstances stiffle us in some way. Or, perhaps someone hurts us by an insensitive remark or action. Or, possibly someone sets out to ruin our reputation with malicious gossip. We can think of hundreds of things that could cause us to be angry. And, I'm sure from our natural, human viewpoint, most of them would be good reasons to get angry. But, not from God's viewpoint!

You'll notice, throughout Jesus' life, He was never angry when personal abuse was heaped upon Him. In fact, He even asked His Father to forgive the people who nailed Him to the cross. He only got angry when someone attacked His Father's character. **As we become more Christ-like, our angry moments will only be when God's reputation is at stake.** He hasn't given us the right to be angry when one of our supposedly natural rights has been violated. As an ambassador for Jesus Christ, we actually have no rights.

Our role is simply to carry out His will. And, the more we see ourselves as Jesus' personal representative in what we're doing, the less reasons we'll have for anger on our own behalf.

So, what do you do in a difficult situation when you'd ordinarily get angry? When you sense that anger emotion beginning to surge, first remember you're an ambassador for Jesus Christ. His reputation is at stake by your remarks and actions. Then, discern the cause of your anger. Is it because something didn't go your way, or is it because God's reputation is being harmed? If God's reputation is at stake, then do as Jesus did. First, get by yourself to determine how you'll approach it in a manner that doesn't violate any of God's values. Then, take action to be sure God's reputation doesn't suffer anymore.

If, on the other hand, you're getting angry because something didn't go your way, then agree with God that your initial response of anger is wrong. You might even have to get off by yourself for awhile and let your emotions settle so you can get the situation in God's perspective again. And, most of the time, our reasons for getting angry is because we consider something is going wrong for us. Those times will become fewer and fewer as we become Christ-like in everything we do.

Focal Point

Emotion of anger.

Christ-Like Response

First, see yourself as an ambassador for Jesus Christ in the situation. Then discern the reason for your anger, and work at seeing the situation from God's perspective.

Possible Identifiers

1. Someone cuts in line ahead of you.

2. You're being constantly interrupted.

3.

4.

5.

6.

"NO ONE CAN SERVE TWO MASTERS; FOR EITHER HE WILL HATE THE ONE AND LOVE THE OTHER, OR HE WILL HOLD TO ONE AND DESPISE THE OTHER. YOU CANNOT SERVE GOD AND MAMMON."

Matthew 6:24

CHAPTER TWENTY-THREE

ASKING FOR ENCOURAGEMENT

Based on Matthew 26:36-41

JESUS IN ACTION

The scene is the Garden of Gethsemane. Jesus could have chosen to face His tremendous ordeal completely alone as He had other difficult situations in the past. But he didn't. He took three of His men with Him and asked them to stay awake and watch. Apparently Jesus felt that His friends' physical presence, and their being aware of His anguish, would give Him encouragement in His time of great need. **He wanted support and asked for it!** With a select few of His companions, Jesus shared His deepest, innermost feelings over His upcoming ordeal. "My soul is deeply grieved, to the point of death," He told His men. "Remain here and keep watch with Me."

PERSONAL APPLICATION

Perhaps you find asking for support from others is against your grain. It can easily open you up for others to see your inner struggles. And, there are times we'd rather not have anyone see what's really going on inside us. Following Jesus' lead in asking for encouragement doesn't mean we have to ask everyone we meet on the street. Jesus didn't. He asked encouragement from three very close friends. It also doesn't mean we should ask for encouragement in everything we do. But, when you have an important decision to make, an awesome task to face, or personal grief to bear, follow Jesus' example and ask a few close friends for their encouragement.

A word of caution might be in order. Be careful not to share anything negative about someone with whom you might be having some problems. Usually when we do that, our desire is more in line with getting things off our chest than it is to receive encouragement in how to handle the situation. God's word tells us to let only those words proceed from our mouth that are good for edification (Ephesians 4:29). **So, be discreet in what you share with your close friends in asking for their encouragement.** Make sure their focus of attention will be on helping you rather than seeing anybody else in an unpleasant light.

Focal Point

Feeling inner turmoil.

Christ-Like Response

Share with close friends your inner struggles. Then, tell them specifically how they can support and encourage you.

Possible Identifiers

1. Facing a difficult decision.

2. Having received bad news.

3. Feeling pressured.

4.

5.

6.

"IF ANY ONE WANTS TO BE FIRST, HE SHALL BE LAST OF ALL, AND SERVANT OF ALL."

Mark 9:35

"FOR WHAT WILL A MAN BE PROFITED, IF HE GAINS THE WHOLE WORLD, AND FORFEITS HIS SOUL? OR WHAT WILL A MAN GIVE IN EXCHANGE FOR HIS SOUL?

Matthew 16:26

CHAPTER TWENTY-FOUR

WHAT TO DO WHEN A FRIEND LETS YOU DOWN
Based on Matthew 26:36-41

JESUS IN ACTION

No sooner had Jesus asked His friends to keep awake and watch with Him, that they fell asleep. Can you believe it? Just when Jesus was facing the most difficult moment He had ever faced! Oh, it was late at night. And it was difficult to stay awake and watch. But, after seeing the great turmoil Jesus was in, you'd think they wouldn't have had that much of a problem in doing it.

How did Jesus handle the situation? When He saw His disciples had let Him down, Jesus could have been filled with self-pity. "Don't they even care about Me in My greatest hour of need?" He could have thought. And, He could have sulked and given them the quiet treatment. **But instead, Jesus took His eyes off Himself, and, while understanding their weakness, He rebuked their actions.** "So, you men could not watch with Me for one hour? Keep watching and praying, that you may not enter into temptation; the spirit is willing, but the flesh is weak."

You'll notice Jesus used a three-step approach in His rebuke to His disciples. First, He let them know of His disappointment ("So, you men could not keep watch with Me for one hour?"). But He didn't belabor His disappointment with them. He quickly explained what they needed to do ("Keep watching and praying, that you may not enter into temptation;"). And, then He let them know He understood them ("The spirit is willing, but the flesh is weak."). Yes, He let them know of His disappointment. But, He also told them what they needed to do to improve as well as let them know He understood them. What a solid combination of actions to take when a friend lets us down!

PERSONAL APPLICATION

Now, what's our natural way of dealing with someone who lets us down? Verbally unload on him? Give him the silent treatment? Or, just let daggers fly from our eyes? All of these reactions would be natural, but not Christ-like. Jesus first communicated the fact of how disappointed He was in them. Then, He gave them a correct course of action to take. Then He let them know He understood them. And, that's what we need to do to represent Jesus Christ to friends who we feel let us down.

Focal Point

Friend who lets you down.

Christ-Like Response

Explain your disappointment in what he did. Then let him know what you expect him to do. Finally, let him know you understand how difficult it might be to do it.

Possible Identifiers

1. Person is late in meeting you.

2. Person didn't do what he promised he'd do.

3.

4.

5.

6.

"BUT I SAY TO YOU, LOVE YOUR ENEMIES, AND PRAY FOR THOSE WHO PERSECUTE YOU IN ORDER THAT YOU MAY BE SONS OF YOUR FATHER WHO IS IN HEAVEN; FOR HE CAUSES HIS SUN TO RISE ON THE EVIL AND THE GOOD AND SENDS RAIN ON THE RIGHTEOUS AND THE UNRIGHTEOUS."

Matthew 5:44-45

"BEWARE OF THE FALSE PROPHETS, WHO COME TO YOU IN SHEEP'S CLOTHING, BUT INWARDLY ARE RAVENOUS WOLVES."

Matthew 7:15

CHAPTER TWENTY-FIVE

HANDLING DIFFERENCES WITH A LEADER

Based on Matthew 26:38-39

JESUS IN ACTION

Nobody could know the agony Jesus was experiencing as He lay flat on His face in the Garden of Gethsemane. With three of His closest friends sound asleep a few steps away, Jesus was alone with His Father! He was facing one of the most cruel ways ever devised to put anyone to death, the crucifixion. It would mean separated shoulders, compressed lungs and shattered nerves. But, it would mean more than that for Jesus. And, it was the "more" He feared the most. Total separation from His Father! You see, His Father had chosen the crucifixion as the means by which Jesus would pay the penalty for all of mankind's sins. But, Jesus didn't want to be separated from His Father. He cringed at the thought of having all of mankind's sins placed on Him. He knew that would thrust Him out of His Father's companionship. And lying in the dirt on that moonlit night, Jesus didn't want to do what His Father had planned for Him.

How did He handle this difference of opinion with His Father? He could have defiantly yelled, "No! I'm not going to do it!" But, instead He tactfully expressed His desire to His Father for another course of action. "If it be possible, let this cup pass from Me..." This "cup" referred to that portion of His life. He wanted to do it another way! **Yet, after expressing His desire, He let the final decision rest with His Father.** "Thy will be done," were His words of commitment to do what His Father wanted. He didn't beg, try to convince or sway His Father. He simply let

His own desires be known, and then let go of His will and committed Himself to whatever His Father wanted done. By doing this, He showed He was committed to carry out His Father's desires, even if they weren't the same as what His first choice would have been.

PERSONAL APPLICATION

What do you do when you differ with a person whose decision affects you, and he's in authority over you? Ridicule or put him down? Some of the most natural reactions are to sulk, pout, argue, withdraw, show anger or use carefully selected sarcasm. Yet, Jesus didn't do any of these. He showed respect for His Father by asking for an alternate plan. At the same time, He communicated an attitude of going along with His Father's final decision. **True submission, as Jesus demonstrated, takes a lot of strength. It means willfully yielding yourself, in your attitude as well as actions, to the control of another person. But, it also includes your privilege of making your desires known!**

We all have opportunities to do this, don't we? Workers don't always agree with their bosses. Children don't always agree with their parents. And, wives don't always agree with their husbands. Anyone can do his own thing. It takes respect for your leader to present to him an alternate plan, or request one from him. And, it takes strength to go with your leader's final decision with a sincere and supportive attitude **even when he might be wrong!**

Here's something important to keep in mind. God can easily change the mind of your leader. So, you can rest in knowing that since God could change your leader's mind, and yet chose not to, that God is working out the results He wants **through** what your leader has asked you to do.

Of course, I'm talking about a decision your leader makes that is consistent with God's ways. **If you're asked to do something inconsistent with God's ways, then you have a responsibility to go to your leader and let him know that you can't do it (Acts 5:29).** Even then, it's wise to go with an alternate plan of action. Most likely, your leader didn't purposely tell you to do something that would violate your convictions. By your desiring to give an alternate plan, or asking for one from him, he'd have an option of either trying an alternate way of doing it or dismissing you from his leadership.

A biblical example of presenting an alternate plan was how Daniel, in the Old Testament, handled his situation when he was told to go against his God's ordinances (Daniel 1:8-21). Submission to someone's authority doesn't mean you blindly do whatever you're asked to do. Jesus was totally submissive to His Father's authority, yet **He expressed to His Father His own personal desires.** In that expression, however, was an attitude of doing whatever His Father finally decided. And, that's what real submission is all about!

Focal Point

Difference of an opinion with a leader.

Christ-Like Response

Show respect for your leader by going to him with a possible alternate course of action, or request one from him. Then, be sure you let your leader know, by your attitude, you'll go with his final decision.

Possible Identifiers

1. A difference of an opinion with your husband.

2. A difference of an opinion with your boss, or your minister.

3.

4.

5.

6.

PART FOUR

PRACTICAL HOW TO'S FOR LIVING THE CHRISTIAN LIFE

CHAPTER TWENTY-SIX

WHAT DO I DO WHEN I DON'T KNOW WHAT TO DO?

What do you do when you don't know what Jesus would do in your situation? Or, what if after learning from the 15 episodes of His life in this book, you still don't remember what He'd do when you encounter similar situations? Not knowing what the Bible says about something in particular can easily happen, can't it? Well, relax. In this chapter we'll explore **two easy-to-remember principles** which you can begin to apply in many situations right now. As you practice them, you can continue to learn from Jesus' life, and the rest of the Bible, what He would have you do in your various activities each day. Although these two principles won't cover everything you face, they're general enough to apply to many of your daily situations. You'll find tear-out sheets for these two principles included in the back of this book to help you remember them.

HOW TO HANDLE DIFFICULT CIRCUMSTANCES

Everyone faces unpleasant circumstances now and then. No one is exempt. Jesus Christ wasn't exempt and neither was the apostle Paul. In fact, Paul experienced shipwrecks, beatings, sleepless nights, and even a stoning. He was thrown into prison several times, and it was from his experience in the Roman prison we have our first principle.

Principle One. Realize that God will use your circumstances to further His purpose as you remain committed to Him and His way.

The apostle Paul displayed this attitude in his Roman imprisonment. And, it was from that prison he wrote to the Christians in Philippi:

> "Now I want you to know, brethren, that my circumstances have turned out for the **greater progress** of the gospel..."
>
> Philippians 1:12

It wasn't fun for Paul to be in prison, but he understood from God's perspective that his imprisonment meant progress for God's purpose. Through his ordeal, others were coming into a knowledge of Jesus Christ. Throughout the day and night Paul was chained to one of the 9000 select Roman soldiers called the praetorian guard. These men were very influential because they had the job of protecting the Emperor. Several of them took turns guarding Paul. And, apparently, he didn't waste any time in seizing opportunities to share with his "captivated" audience how Jesus loved them and died in payment for their sins. Each of these guards must have seen in Paul the reality of which he was speaking. Soon, the "chain reaction" took place and news of Jesus spread throughout the entire praetorian guard! Difficult circumstances? Sure they were! But God enabled Paul to rise above his rough times and to rely on God to further His purpose through them. Not only did Paul's imprisonment get the good news about Jesus to the Roman guards, but his difficult circumstances enabled Paul to write letters to the Christians in Philippi, and other places. Paul never saw God's full purpose in his imprisonment. But, God is still using Paul's prison letters to teach Christians everywhere how to live a more Christ-like life.

Personal Application. Some of your circumstances aren't very good either, are they? Perhaps you've got a deadline to meet and you catch the flu. Maybe you're given a surprise exam and all you know is your name. Or, perhaps your newly planted garden gets uprooted by a downpour of rain. You might even be suffering from a disease, or you might be disabled. All difficult circumstances to one degree or another! In such times it's easy to complain, become discouraged and even doubt that God loves you. Well, Paul had many opportunities to feel that way. But, he didn't. **In spite of his circumstances he thanked God (1 Thessalonians 5:18). Paul relied on God working out His purpose through his difficult times, and in spite of them (Romans 8:28)!** And, He'll do the same in your circumstances. You don't have to know **how** God will produce His results, or even what results He's working on. Just know **He's going to do it** because His word promises it.

RELATIONSHIPS WITH PEOPLE

Another area common to all of us is our relating to other people. We live in a world full of people and most of us will be relating to hundreds of them during our lifetime. This second principle will help us relate to them in a Christ-like way.

Principle Two. Take every opportunity to look for ways you can serve others.

What made the apostle Paul so well liked by other people? Well, one of the things that stands out in his letters is his tremendous concern for other people. He explained his approach to other people, and the approach we should take, this way.

> "Do nothing from selfishness or empty conceit, but with humility of mind let each of you regard one another as **more important** than

himself; do not merely look out for your own personal interests, but also for the interests of others."

Philippians 2:3-4

Most of us want to be important, don't we? We want to be valued by other people and we want them to like us. We want to feel we have something worthwhile to contribute. Our focus is pretty much on ourselves. And, our natural self-centeredness can tell us to look out for ourselves, because no one else will. Many of us do just that. We want the most, the biggest and the best for ourselves. We'd choose to be the guest of honor rather than be just an invited guest. We'd rather be on the top of the sales chart than be one of the many names below. We'd rather be served than serve. Well, if anyone had a right to be served, it was Jesus! Yet, He said He came to serve rather than be served (Matthew 20:28). And, His actions backed it up! He healed hundreds of people throughout His ministry, went against the accepted "hands off" policy regarding the dreaded lepers, got down on His hands and knees to wash His disciples' dirty feet and then endured a torturous death on our behalf. **Throughout His life we catch this one basic theme, sacrifice of His own comfort for the benefit of others.**

Personal Application. From a human perspective, you have rights the same as anyone else does. A husband might feel he should have the right to come home from work and relax. After all, his job is over. He's earned the pay that day and now has a right to rest. A wife might feel she has a right to have her husband help her once he gets home. Her job is never over. And, she has a right to rest just as much as her husband does.

Well, you can't be Christ-like by clinging to your natural rights. Jesus didn't cling to His rights and neither did the apostle Paul. Can you imagine what would happen throughout our troubled world if everyone considered other people to be more important than themselves? No wars. No stealings. No murders. No crime at all! Unrealistic? Perhaps, but let's narrow it down by just considering how such an attitude would affect your family life. Wouldn't it be fantastic? No family quarrels. More togetherness. Why, you'd be looking for ways to help each member of your family as well as take care of your own needs. And that, my friend, can happen! It depends on your commitment to do it and the Holy Spirit helping you get it done. It might mean a husband helping his wife with the dishes. It might mean a wife shining her husband's shoes. Or, it might mean both of them giving each other a nice backrub.

You can become more Christ-like, as you're empowered by the Holy Spirit, by setting your mind on seeing others as more important than yourself. Refuse to cling to your own natural rights. When you do this, you'll begin to look for ways to help other people instead of expecting others to serve you.

What do you do when you don't know what Jesus would do? You'll be encouraged to see how often one of these two principles from Philippians applies throughout your day. And, as you set your mind on applying them, you'll be doing exactly what Jesus would do in your situation!

FOR INDEPENDENT AND GROUP STUDY

1. What are two difficult circumstances you face in your home, work or school?

2. In what way does the command to give thanks in all things (1 Thessalonians 5:18) help in dealing with difficult circumstances?

3. Can you sincerely be thankful in the circumstances you just mentioned, or would it just be lip service? Please explain.

4. Discuss three specific situations at home and work in which you can apply the principle from Philippians 2:3-4.

5. In what ways will you see people you mentioned in the three situations as more important than yourself?

"THEREFORE, WE ARE AMBASSADORS FOR CHRIST, AS THOUGH GOD WERE ENTREATING THROUGH US; WE BEG YOU ON BEHALF OF CHRIST, BE RECONCILED TO GOD."

2 Corinthians 5:20

CHAPTER TWENTY-SEVEN

BUT I DON'T WANT TO DO AS JESUS WOULD DO!

Although we have various reasons for not wanting to do what Jesus would do, the reason I'll be dealing with in this chapter is when we're **emotionally upset.** You've had moments when you've been emotionally upset, haven't you? Perhaps it was caused by a communications breakdown. Or, you might have just received bad news. During those moments, you might have lost your desire to do what Jesus would do. Ordinarily you want to do things His way, but not when your nerve endings are on fire! We all have moments like these. How do we deal with them when they come? In this brief chapter I'd like to share two steps I usually take during these emotionally upsetting moments that have helped me come back with a determination to do what pleases Jesus.

1. **Stabilize your emotions.** If this means getting off by yourself awhile, do it. No, you don't have to leave town. And, you might not even have to leave your house. But, try to get off where you don't have to talk to anyone. If your emotions will stabilize faster when other people are around, then try to get with other people. The important thing is to bring your emotions back to an even keel in a Christ-like way. Then, you'll be in a position to take the second step.

2. **After your emotions have stabilized, begin doing what you know Jesus would do.** You don't have to be enthusiastic. Just begin. As you do, the Holy Spirit will renew your enthusiasm to please Jesus. But, you must take that first step, even when you don't feel like it!

Oh, one more thing. There's no need to get down on yourself when you don't feel like doing what Jesus wants you to do.

Just realize the moment will pass and you'll regain your enthusiasm.

"BE ANXIOUS FOR NOTHING, BUT IN EVERYTHING BY PRAYER AND SUPPLICATION WITH THANKSGIVING LET YOUR REQUESTS BE MADE KNOWN TO GOD. AND THE PEACE OF GOD, WHICH SURPASSES ALL COMPRE— HENSION, SHALL GUARD YOUR HEARTS AND YOUR MINDS IN CHRIST JESUS."

Philippians 4:6-7

"WHATEVER YOU DO, DO YOUR WORK HEARTILY, AS FOR THE LORD RATHER THAN FOR MEN; KNOWING THAT FROM THE LORD YOU WILL RECEIVE THE REWARD OF THE INHERITANCE. IT IS THE LORD CHRIST WHOM YOU SERVE."

Colossians 3:23-24

CHAPTER TWENTY-EIGHT

ESTABLISHING CHRIST-LIKE OBJECTIVES AND SCHEDULING

You'll find some of the ideas expressed to you in this book new and challenging. And, you'll want to try and incorporate them into your daily walk with Jesus. But if you don't have a plan to work these principles into your life, chances are they'll lie dormant in this book and put away on a shelf. That's why so many Christians feel they live "wasted" days. **They don't incorporate those things into their lives they know they should be doing.** Without careful planning, the convictions you feel strongly about today can quietly recede into the background, and your life will be no different than before you picked up this book to read. To get these truths into your life, it'll take planning. First, by **establishing**

Christ-like objectives, and then by **scheduling** them on a daily basis.

I remember a conversation I had with a friend who dropped over to our house one evening. He explained how frustrated he was because it seemed he just wasn't getting things done during the day. "How much time do you take to schedule your activities?" I asked. "None," was his reply. "Well, have you ever taken time to think through what objectives you should pursue throughout your lifetime, as well as on a daily basis?" "What do you mean by that?" he questioned. Then, I showed him my little pocket diary in which most of my activities for the day were scheduled. I told him these specific activities were in line with several Christ-like objectives I was working towards. "It's not just a matter of putting a lot of things down to be done each day," I told him. "You have to put the right things down, things that would line up with what Jesus would do in your situation." Immediately my friend's expression changed as he began to see how he could be more effective.

Now, my friend's problem might not be the same one you face. He didn't feel he was getting enough things done during the day. Perhaps you're on the other end of the spectrum. You might always be on the go, but wonder if your time is used to its best advantage. In this chapter, we'll explore a very effective way in dealing with both problems. We'll see how you can develop some lifetime, or long-range, objectives and then some short-range objectives you can schedule on a daily basis.

If your greatest desire is to become Christ-like in everything you do, then you must have Christ-like objectives. A Christ-like objective is simply something you work towards that keeps you in line with your overall goal of being Christ-like. It's a matter of involving yourself in doing those things Jesus would be doing in your place each day. You can use the following three steps, in the same manner as my friend did, to help develop clear, Christ-like objectives.

SELECTING CHRIST-LIKE OBJECTIVES

1. On paper, divide your life into the various roles you have. For instance, some of your different roles could include being a husband, wife, parent, student, employer, employee, homemaker, deacon, Girl Scout leader, member of the local church, pastor, etc. By first defining the various roles you have, it'll be easier to determine what Jesus would do in each of them. Once you've listed your roles, you're ready to take the next step to determine some general objectives.

2. Now, select long-range objectives for each of your roles. A long-range objective is what Jesus would do in each of the roles you have. In other words, what would He want you to do as a husband, wife, parent, student, Bible study leader, pastor, etc? **Your long-range objectives answer the question, "What would Jesus want done?"** The answer to that question usually can't be measured on a daily basis. For instance, one of your long-range objectives, in your role as a husband, might be to develop better personal communication with your wife. As a student, a long-range objective might be to develop better study habits. You wouldn't really be able to measure either of those objectives on a daily basis, would you? They're things you work towards, and by developing them, you'll become more Christ-like.

Now, you might not always know what Jesus would want you to do in each of your roles. So, put down on paper what you think He'd want you to do. And then, examine what you've put down by asking if it's in any way offensive to any of the values Jesus taught. **If you have any doubt about what you've put down, it's best to leave it out.** Reading Jesus' Sermon on the Mount, in Matthew 5-7, will help you evaluate whether or not your long-range objectives are in line with those Jesus would have for you. For example, setting a specific financial level you want to earn, as a long-range objective, might well be in conflict with Jesus' teaching against laying up for yourselves treasures on earth (Matthew 6:19). Now, the more you get to know God's word, the easier it'll be to know what long-range objectives are valid for each role.

3. Select short-range objectives to help you reach each long-range objective. A short-range objective is how Jesus would do something. It can always be **measured and scheduled** on your daily calendar. And, it must always relate to a corresponding long-range objective. Let's say one of your long-range objectives is to develop better communication with your wife. A short-range objective might be to set aside the first ten minutes when you get home each evening to discuss with her things that have happened in her life that day. That short-range objective is tangible and will help you reach your long-range objective of developing better communication with her. You can schedule ten minutes each day to do it. **Whereas your long-range objectives ask what would Jesus do in each of your roles, your short-range objectives tell how He would do it in your particular situation.**

A SAMPLE WORKSHEET

Now, let's walk through a sample worksheet to get a better idea of how each step ties together. For the sake of illustration we'll just use the roles of a husband and a wife.

Role: Being A Husband

Long-range Objectives (What would Jesus do?)	Short-range Objectives (How would Jesus do it?)
1. Develop better communication with my wife. (1 Corinthians 1:10 and 2 Corinthians 13:11)	1. I'll spend the first ten minutes with my wife when I come home each day talking to her about her activities. This will be a time when I'll try to understand her feelings better. 2. I'll spend a half hour reading a book with my wife on two separate evenings each week. 3. I'll spend a few minutes three times a week praying with my wife concerning various things on our minds.

Role: Being A Wife

Long-range Objectives
(What would Jesus do?)

1. Understand my husband's interests.

   (Philippians 2:3-4)

2. Cultivate romance with my wife.

   (1 Corinthians 7:3-5 and Song of Solomon)

   1. I'll take my wife out on a date twice a month to do something she'd like to do.

   2. I'll spend a weekend away with my wife every other month.

   3. I'll get a good book on romantic love, as it's explained in the Song of Solomon, and cultivate that type of romance in our marriage.

Short-range Objectives
(How would Jesus do it?)

1. I'll ask my husband questions about his work each evening. But I'll need to understand if he's tired and doesn't care to talk about his work at that time.

2. I'll browse through publications concerning his work one evening a week.

Continued from last page

3. I'll ask my husband's opinion on the different clothes I wear.

2. Develop a romantic atmosphere for my husband.

(1 Corinthians 7:3-5 and Song of Solomon)

1. I'll have the house cleaned up before he gets home from work each day.

2. I'll ask him what he'd like to have for dinner at least once a week, and prepare it for him.

3. I'll praise him concerning one of his good qualities every night.

4. I'll take a shower and freshen up early in the evening at least three nights a week.

THREE GUIDELINES

Now, you can see, we haven't exhausted either the long-range objectives or their respective short-range objectives under these two roles. But, this will give you an idea how to develop the rest of your long-range and short-range objectives on paper. Here are three guidelines to keep in mind as you take on this interesting project.

1. Plan on using at least two full evenings to establish your Christ-like objectives for all of your roles.

2. Discuss your particular objectives with your spouse, if you're married, so you can help each other work towards their fulfillment.

3. If you don't know for sure what objectives Jesus would have in each of your roles, put down what you think is best. Then evaluate them in view of what Jesus taught. His Sermon on the Mount is a good place to start. Remember, the more intimately you know Him, the easier it'll be to know what He'd do in your various roles.

SCHEDULING YOUR OBJECTIVES

Establishing Christ-like objectives is an important step in doing away with those "wasted" days. Now, having objectives in your mind is fine, but they'll do you more good when you schedule them on a daily basis. **Remember, it's only your short-range objectives that can be scheduled.** One of the things you should consider buying is a good daily and weekly reminder. The one I use is called the Mini Star Diary System, and you can receive information on it by sending your request to Global Sales Corporation, P.O.Box 15551, Santa Ana, CA 92705. It's much easier to do things the way Jesus Christ would in your various roles when you have them scheduled on a daily basis. Here's a sample of how a weekly schedule might look if some of the husband's short-range objectives, from our sample worksheet, were scheduled for a one week period.

A SAMPLE SCHEDULE IS ON THE NEXT PAGE.

SAMPLE SCHEDULE

SUNDAY

8:00 p.m. --
Read book with Peggy, and then pray with her.

MONDAY

5:30 p.m. --
Talk to Peggy about her day.

TUESDAY

5:30 p.m. --
Talk to Peggy about her day.

WEDNESDAY

5:30 p.m. --
Talk to Peggy about her day.
8:00 p.m. --
Pray with Peggy.

THURSDAY

5:30 p.m. --
Talk to Peggy about her day.
8:00 p.m. --
Read book with Peggy.

FRIDAY

8:00 p.m. --
Pray with Peggy.

SATURDAY

8:00 a.m. --
Leave with Peggy for Phoenix.

Of course, you'd also have several other short-range objectives scheduled as they relate to your various roles. Although you'll immediately experience a more meaningful use of your time by scheduling your short-range objectives, let me caution you on **a possible danger** in too rigidly following your schedule. **You can become more schedule-oriented than Christ-oriented.** This danger was brought to my attention when I was in seminary. I've always enjoyed getting things done, and in my seminary days I had each day completely scheduled. If anything interfered with my schedule, I'd become frustrated. For instance, if I had planned on so much time to study, and someone would just want to casually talk, I'd get tense as I'd look for an opening to get away from the person. Then one day, as our seminary librarian tried to talk to me on my way to a table, he noticed I wasn't really paying attention to what he was saying. "You know, Wes," he said as I was edging my way to the table, "a person can be such a slave to his schedule he's no longer sensitive to what pleases God." "I know," I replied as I moved on. "It's a shame when people let that happen to them." Then, as I hurried off to work on my project, I realized he was describing me! It hit me hard how insensitive I had become. Fortunately, God has given us the proper balance in what our attitude should be toward scheduling. And, I now try to keep that balance in mind as I carry out my responsibilities.

> "Come now, you who say 'Today or tomorrow, we shall go to such and such a city, and spend a year there and engage in business and make a profit.' Yet you do not know what your life will be like tomorrow. You are just a vapor that appears for a little while and then vanishes away. Instead, you ought to say, **'If the Lord wills,** we shall live and also do this or that.'"
>
> James 4:13-15

"If the Lord wills" is the key phrase. Your schedule is to help you do those things Jesus would do in your place. However, God might have something other than what you have scheduled in mind. **When an "interruption" comes, try to evaluate it from God's viewpoint.** How would Jesus handle it if He were in your shoes? The more you get to know Him, the easier it'll be to make such an evaluation. If you discern that the "interruption" is sent by God, then you need to direct your attention entirely to it. There were times, in my seminary days, when I couldn't afford to casually talk to someone when my studies had a higher priority. But, there were other times, such as when I rushed off to the library table, when it would have been a higher priority to talk to someone. Our seminary librarian would agree with that!

Just as the Sabbath was made for man, and not man for the Sabbath, so is your schedule made for you. It's to help you become **more productive** in the priorities Jesus would have in your various roles. It's not to enslave you so you become insensitive to what God has already planned for you that day.

IT'S OUR RESPONSIBILITY!

But, in spite of this danger of becoming schedule-oriented rather than Christ-oriented, daily scheduling your short-range objectives is one of the most important things you can do to make the most of your time and guard against those "wasted" days. Time is something you can never relive. And, how you use it will count for eternity. **As an ambassador for Jesus Christ, you have a responsibility to Him to use your time the same way He would in your place.**

FOR INDEPENDENT AND GROUP STUDY

1. What is a long range objective and how does it relate to your goal of being Christ-like?

2. How do short range objectives relate to your long range objectives?

3. Why is it important to write out your Christ-like objectives?

4. Why can't your long range objectives be put on a daily schedule?

5. Select long range objectives for three of your roles.

6. Select short range objectives for each of the long range objectives you just selected.

7. What is a potential danger in scheduling your activities each day?

8. How can you guard against that danger?

9. Purchase a daily and weekly reminder and begin scheduling your Christ-like short range objectives.

"AND WHATEVER YOU DO IN WORD OR DEED, DO ALL IN THE NAME OF THE LORD JESUS, GIVING THANKS THROUGH HIM TO GOD THE FATHER."

Colossians 3:17

CHAPTER TWENTY-NINE

DEVELOPING WILLPOWER

"I know what to do, but I just don't do it!" "Someday I'm going to get organized!" "I want to lose 15 pounds so badly, but I just can't seem to stop eating!" "Why can't I get up early enough each day to read some of God's word?" Do any of these statements sound familiar to you? Maybe you've heard someone else make them, or perhaps you've made them yourself.

Honest desires? Sure they are. The wishing is there, but the doing isn't. Not because you don't want to do them. But, somewhere between "I'm going to do it" and actually doing them, there's a breakdown. A 20-day diet survives three days. You get up early enough to read God's word four days in a row. But, you're rushed the fifth day, and.... Well, you know the rest of the story. So what's the problem? Call it a lack of discipline, or a lack of willpower, or a lack of self-control. **This is one of the biggest hindrances a Christian has in becoming Christ-like.**

Most of us don't lack willpower in all the areas of our lives, do we? It's just in a few important ones. And we struggle in these areas year after year hoping to make some progress. We all have them. Weaknesses in being overweight, in being consistently late, in driving over the speed limit, in cutting in when others are talking or in talking too much ourselves, never getting around to fix things, putting off shopping for Christmas or birthday gifts until the last minute, neglecting to keep up on our correspondence, watching unedifying TV programs, etc. You get the idea. All areas in which we're frustrated and not very Christ-like.

OUR IDEAL MOTIVATION

Becoming Christ-like in those areas isn't automatic, is it? We intellectually know that the Holy Spirit could transform us, even in those weak areas, if we'd only consciously do as Jesus would do each moment. But that takes willpower to consciously work with Him in those areas of defeat. And, that's our problem. Our willpower just isn't strong enough to consistently do things God's way. What's the answer? How can we develop our willpower? **The apostle Paul has an answer for us. He explained that His love for Jesus was his motivation.** He wrote, "For the love of Christ controls us..." (2 Corinthians 5:14).

"Controls" here describes what a nozzle does to water coming out of a hose. It channels the water and thrusts it out of the hose with a new force so it makes a greater impact where it's directed. That's how Paul described what his love for Jesus did for him. **It channeled his energies to do things that would be pleasing to Jesus rather than himself.** We see from his life many examples of this. Paul had plenty of opportunities to give in to his own desires for personal safety, companionship, etc. But for the cause of Christ he knowingly went into situations that resulted in several imprisonments, beatings, stonings and shipwrecks. He was even in the water twenty four hours one time rather than seek his own comfort (2 Corinthians 11:23-25).

Paul's life is an example to us of willpower. And, we're commanded to imitate Paul as he imitated Christ (1 Corinthians 11:1). No, that doesn't mean we have to be shipwrecked some place or even thrown into prison. It just means we need to be willing and determined to go through hardships, in line with doing what Jesus would do, rather than give in to our natural desires. Our hardships might mean less sleep, less food, less TV, etc. Paul was able to endure his hardships because of his love for the Lord. And, that's the ideal motive for us doing as Jesus would do. **Our motive should be to do what we know is pleasing to Jesus as our expression of love for Him.**

A MIDDLE STEP

"Well, I guess I don't love Him enough, or I'd do those things I know He wants me to do," I can hear you say. "But isn't there something I can do while my love for the Lord increases? For instance, when I'm 15 pounds overweight and see a hot-fudge sundae, I'm not thinking about my love for Jesus. I'm thinking about how good the sundae will taste! Or, when the alarm goes off in the morning, I'm only thinking about how sleepy I am. I'm not showing my love for Jesus by getting up and spending time with Him by reading the Bible."

Isn't the same true in all of our weak areas? **At a particular moment our desire to do what we want to do outweighs our desire to do what we know we should do.** Our natural tendency is to do what's immediately pleasing to us, rather than what's pleasing to the Lord. Well, hang on. There's a solution. No, I'm not going to tell you simply to do it. If it was that easy, you'd already be doing everything pleasing to Jesus. Let's look at some advice Paul wrote to his young protege, Timothy, that will give some insight into how our willpower can be developed.

> "...on the other hand, **discipline yourself** for the purpose of **godliness;** for bodily discipline is only of little profit, but godliness is profitable for all things..."
>
> 1 Timothy 4:7-8

A NEW FOCUS

Did you catch the reason Paul told Timothy to be disciplined, or have willpower? To become godly. That's the same as becoming Christ-like, and it's a different reason than we usually have for wanting to improve our weak areas, isn't it? Our natural tendency might be to want to lose 15 pounds because we want to look better in our clothes, or on the beach. A good reason, but we're doing it more for self-satisfaction than for godliness. And, that's the wrong focus. **So, the first thing we need to understand, before we can develop our willpower, is our focus has to be changed from a self-satisfaction to a Christ-satisfaction.** The purpose for losing those 15 pounds needs to be changed from looking good in our clothes, or on the beach, to developing godliness, or Christ-likeness!

And, that's the new twist. **Instead of losing 15 pounds simply to look good, you'll lose them as a result of developing your willpower to become more Christ-like.** For example, let's say you desire to bring your eating habits in line with what Jesus would have you do. You realize you've been feeding your self-centeredness by giving in to your desire for sweet foods. And, by giving in to your desire in this area time after time, you're creating an attitude where you want to be satisfied in other things as well. You're becoming inwardly-directed. And, that's not Christ-like. So, you decide to eliminate cookies, cake, ice cream, jellies, etc. from your daily diet. Oh, you might have them occasionally when you eat out, but they're no longer a part of your daily habit. You're doing this because you want to develop your willpower to say "No" to self and "Yes" to Christ. As your willpower is being developed into godliness, what do you suppose happens to those 15 excessive pounds? They just seem to vanish, don't they? In the process of becoming stronger-willed for more godliness, you now fit into your clothes, and look good on the beach as well.

IT TAKES TIME

From this same scripture, God gives us other insights in how our willpower can be developed to bring about godliness. **First, we're to discipline ourselves.** Your discipline isn't going to come from a friend, or an instructor, or your spouse, etc. It has to come from you. No one else can do it for you. **Secondly, "discipline" means to exercise or train one's self.** Many years in athletic competition have helped me understand any training program takes time. Every workout is designed to further develop one's physical and mental skills. **Strengthening our will to do things pleasing to Jesus also takes time, and a training program!** With the idea in mind of developing our willpower to become more Christ-like, rather than doing it just for some immediate tangible results, let's explore a training program to strengthen our willpower to more consistently choose to do things the way Jesus would in our place.

THE CREATIVE REWARD SYSTEM

I used to wonder, when I participated in competitive athletics, why I seemed to have the willpower to never miss a strenuous workout, but no willpower when it came to staying away from "junk" foods. It seemed to be so inconsistent. Here I was seemingly so disciplined in one area and so weak-willed in another. Then I discovered something about myself. I realized I was being consistent after all, because both athletics and "junk" food made me feel good. It wasn't that I was really disciplined in athletics, but I kept at it because I enjoyed the rewards I could receive by doing well. Trophies, trips and recognition! And, when it came to eating "junk" foods, I ate them because I liked the taste. I participated in athletics, as well as ate "junk" foods, because I enjoyed the rewards from them.

And, that's the principle upon which this simple, yet effective, Creative Reward System is based. **You desire a certain reward so you discipline yourself to do certain things to get it.** Here's basically how it works. You sign a "contract" in which you commit yourself to do certain things, and refrain from doing other things. A sample contract is included in the tear-out section in the back of this book. You get a point each day you succeed in doing everything, but you lose two points each day you omit any one thing. Now, when you accumulate a selected number of points, you can collect your reward.

For example, I wanted to spend a fun weekend away with my wife. I used that as my reward. The areas in which I wanted to develop stronger willpower on a daily basis, toward more godliness, were: doing stretching and physical fitness exercises, dental flossing my teeth, refraining from eating any sugar foods and refraining from eating more than two pieces of bread a day. It was really fun putting down that one point for each day I was successful. Yes, I had to subtract two points one day. But I was determined to keep going on to get my reward. Sounds simple? It is, and that's why it works. Let's break it down into it's various components and you'll see how simple, yet effective, it really is.

1. Identify areas of weakness in which you want to become more Christ-like. Perhaps you'll want to select areas dealing with food. You'll reward yourself for not eating any sweets or more than two pieces of bread a day. Or, you might want to reward yourself for eating certain foods each day such as fruits and vegetables. Maybe an area for you would be getting proper physical exercise, being prompt, or limiting your TV watching. Perhaps it'll be in getting into God's word and having a time to be with the Lord in prayer each day. It can be any number of things in which you have trouble in consistently doing as Jesus would do. Here are a couple of guidelines to help you get started:

A. Select only things to do, or refrain from doing, that can be **measured on a daily basis.** For instance, your desire to lose 15 pounds wouldn't be valid, because you wouldn't lose those pounds in one day. They'll be lost as a result of other tangible things you do, such as eliminating certain foods from your diet, as well as getting proper physical exercise. This program is based on **specific things** you do, or refrain from doing, just as Jesus would if He was in your situation.

B. For your first training program select no more than **two or three things** over which you want to develop stronger willpower. As in any training program, it's wise to break in easy for the best consistent development to take place.

C. It's also best to **select less problematic areas** for your first program. For instance, if you're weak at being on time as well as undisciplined in eating habits, it might be wise to tackle the promptness problem first. Or if you'd like to tackle the eating problem, just tackle one phase of undisciplined eating, such as limiting yourself to two slices of bread a day, rather than dealing with everything you should do right off the bat. The idea of this Creative Reward System is to build upon success. And since it takes time to develop strong willpower, you'll want to tackle only those areas you can handle more easily than the rest. As your willpower strengthens, you'll be able to handle more glaring weaknesses in your next training program.

2. Determine the number of points you want to accumulate in order to obtain your creative reward. Let's review the point system. You put down one point on your contract everyday you do the things you're supposed to do in your training program. You put down a minus two points if you fail to do any of them. So, by not doing what you should do, it's a difference of three points, the one you would have earned and the two you lost. How many points should you select for your first program? **I suggest 14 as a reasonable number.** It's not too many, but just enough to present a challenge. By earning a point each day, you could receive your reward in two weeks. Then, after seeing how your initial program goes, you can adjust the points for the next one.

3. Select your creative reward. It's called a "creative" reward because it'll take some creativity on your part to come up with one that's appealing, realistic and Christ-like. So, let's explore three guidelines that'll help you choose the right one for each program.

A. Make sure your reward has more **appeal** to you than the things you must discipline yourself to do. For instance, if you're limiting yourself to two pieces of bread a day, make sure your reward is more appealing than that third piece of bread. **Make it something you'd like, but can't have until you earn your points.**

B. Your reward must be **realistic.** A trip to Hawaii most likely is unrealistic because you probably would neither have the money, nor the time, to take the trip. Instead of a trip to Hawaii, a weekend away with your wife, or husband, might be more realistic. Or, you might select a tool you've been wanting, or a new dress that's within your budget. It might even be a night out at your favorite dining spot.

C. Select only a reward that's in line with **what Jesus would select for you.** For instance, if you're trying to stay away from sugar foods, Jesus wouldn't then treat you to a hot-fudge sundae. God's word tells us our body is a temple and we're to care for it. Also, studies have shown that sugar is one of the main causes of disease. If it's difficult to know exactly what Jesus would select, I suggest selecting only those rewards that, in your opinion, don't conflict with any values He taught.

MOST FREQUENTLY ASKED QUESTIONS

Now that you've got a look at how the Creative Reward System works, let's deal with some questions that might be on your mind.

1. What would prevent me from getting my reward without accumulating the necessary points?

Actually, the only reason you'd have for being tempted to get your reward, without earning it, is that you've lost so many points it looks like a lost cause. This really shouldn't happen, if you work on two or three easier areas in your first training program. When I asked one person how he was doing in his program, he replied, "Great, I'm on the plus side!" He told me he had lost a few points, but he knew the program wasn't over until he accumulated his 14 points. So, he took it as a challenge to keep going. And everyday that he accumulated one more point, his willpower got stronger.

2. Can I change my program once it starts?

It's best not to change it, even for upgrading purposes. If you do, you'll find it's easier to change anytime you want to satisfy your natural desires. For example, let's say you want to add another Christ-like thing to do. Instead of adding it to your current program, wait and include it in your next program. You can still do it on a daily basis without having it count for points at the present time.

3. If I eliminate sugar foods as one of my areas to develop willpower, couldn't I become offensive to someone who has invited me over for dinner?

The idea of this training program is to develop willpower to help you become more Christ-like, not leave a bad impression with your hostess. One way to deal with such a problem is to state certain exceptions on your contract before you begin. For instance, if you've chosen to eliminate sugar foods from your diet, you can make an exception when you're invited out to dinner, or on family birthdays. You'd still get your point for the day, providing you'd do the other things. Now, because this program is to help you become more Christ-like as your primary objective, you probably want to limit the number of times each week you go out for dinner. And it's important for any exception to be stated on your contract before you begin your program.

4. I've got my mind on so many things during the day, how can I remember to do what I'm supposed to do?

It's best to have your contract in a place where you can easily keep record of your points. That, in itself, will keep your training program on your mind. A good place might be on your desk at work, or in your bathroom where you get ready for work and bed. Or, you might want to hang it on your refrigerator, especially if you include any type of diet in your training program.

5. Can't I lose heart if I lose too many points?

That can happen, especially if you're thinking more about the points than you are your creative reward, or the reason why you're in the program. Remember, developing willpower takes time. You don't want to lose points, but when it happens you'll see how fun it is to get them back, and continue to work for more.

6. Isn't there a danger of reverting back to old habits once my training program has been completed?

Anytime we don't consciously do things the way Jesus would, we'll do things our natural way (Isaiah 55:8-9 and Colossians 3:2). So, the danger is always present. It'll never be natural to do things God's way. However, as your willpower gains in strength, it'll be easier to commit yourself to do what you know Jesus would do in your situation. I think you'll find it's a good idea to include certain areas from one training program to the next. For instance, if you've been having trouble being on time, you might include promptness in two or three programs in a row. The more you practice something, the easier it'll be to do.

7. I can see the benefits of using a creative reward. But, isn't there a danger I'll end up just working for the reward rather than doing the things because I want to become more Christlike? How do I begin exercising my willpower as an expression of my love for Jesus and not just to get the reward?

Although the Creative Reward System is a transitional training program to have more willpower to do as Jesus would do, there's a danger in just doing what our program calls for to get a reward. One thing I've done to keep the right motive in front of me is to talk to Jesus as I do the things in my program. For instance, as I refrain from eating a piece of pie I want, I might say, "Not eating this pie is an expression of my love for You, Jesus!" I've personally found a simple prayer, like this one, helps me keep the right perspective on why I'm doing it.

This Creative Reward System isn't an end in itself. It's only a stepping stone to help strengthen our willpower. It's a transitional program to get us to the point where we'll desire to do what Jesus wants us to do **with our only reward of pleasing Him!**

FOR INDEPENDENT AND GROUP STUDY

1. What would you consider to be a good definition of willpower?

2. What should be our purpose for developing stronger willpower?

3. Name three specific areas in your life in which you'd like to develop stronger willpower.

4. What is a Creative Reward System? How does it work?

5. What are some possible creative rewards you can use that qualify as appealing, realistic and Christ-like?

6. Using an area from question three, develop a training program with the Creative Reward System. If possible, select someone who would also like to use the system to encourage each other as you begin your first training program.

7. How does developing stronger willpower relate to being a personal ambassador for Jesus Christ?

CHAPTER THIRTY

PREPARING FOR THE DAY

Hollis raced through his house gathering things he had to take to the office. In a whirl he kissed his wife, rushed out the back door, jumped into his car and screeched out the driveway. An unusual morning? Nope! Typical all the way.

"Man, I've got only twenty minutes before the meeting starts," he thought to himself. "It takes me that long just to get there! I hope Ann put that report in my briefcase."

"Oh no! A traffic jam up ahead!" Tenseness etched across Hollis' face as his knuckles turned white clinging to the

steering wheel. "Now I'll never make it on time! This is all I needed!" He sees an opening to the right and cuts in front of another car just barely making the off ramp. "I'll cut through some of these back streets and maybe save some time," he thought to himself.

As Hollis sped down the back streets he looked in his rear view mirror and saw what he feared, a flashing red light. Fuming, he pulled over, slumped down into his seat and tapped his fingers angrily on the steering wheel.

"Hello sir. May I see your driver's license please?" asked the officer. "Yeah," replied Hollis. "Get on with it. I haven't got all day! Say, don't you guys have any criminals to chase?"

THE PROBLEM

Now, Hollis really wasn't as much a victim of his circumstances as he was a victim of his own **lack of preparing** to do things Jesus' way. He might even have seemed like a very committed Christian when all of his circumstances were right. But you never could have convinced the policeman of that. Hollis, like so many of us, didn't prepare adequately to have Christ-like attitudes throughout his day.

My need for such mental preparation was made clear to me after losing a tennis match to a close friend I thought I could easily beat. Although I entered the match with the general attitude of wanting to have the same attitudes Jesus would have throughout the competition, by the end of play I was upset and even a little embarrassed to be beaten. After thinking it through, I realized it was because of poor preparation on my part. **I had deceived myself.** My motives at the beginning of play weren't what I had thought they were on the surface. I was more interested in winning the game than in how I played it. Before our next match I mentally prepared to have Christ-like attitudes in various situations I knew I was going to face. **What a difference that preparation made!** I was really conscious of how I thought Jesus would handle most of my situations throughout the match. Instead of arguing over close calls, I was determined to know the truth. So, if my friend had a better angle of seeing whether the ball was in or out of play, I'd go with his call. If I had a better angle, I'd diplomatically tell him. But instead of arguing I'd suggest we play it again. Instead of getting upset when I'd miss a shot, I'd think through what I could do to improve the next time and continue to play. It was a refreshing experience and quite a bit different than our first match.

THE SOLUTION

God tells us in Isaiah 55:8-9, that our thoughts aren't the same as His thoughts and that our actions also fall short. I can identify with that. Can't you? That's why, unless I'm mentally prepared to handle my daily situations, the same way I prepared for that second tennis match, it's very difficult to have Christ's attitudes. For instance, when I'm tired at the end of the day, it isn't natural to spend time playing with my two girls or spend quality time communicating with my wife. But, by mentally preparing beforehand I've found I'm more alert to do what I think Jesus would do when I get home. And, one of the most effective things I do to start each day is follow a four-step mental preparation program. Perhaps you'll find these steps just as helpful as I have.

1. Write down four or five situations you think you'll encounter during the day. Driving in traffic. Disciplining your kids. Fixing the car. Working on business projects. Talking on the telephone. Cleaning the house. Preparing meals. Talking with people. Attending classes. Doing homework. Being interrupted. Being interrupted? Yes, one of the most annoying situations for most of us is having our mind set on doing something, but being interrupted while doing it. Plan for those interruptions. You'll be able to handle them easier if you plan how to respond to them before they occur.

2. Think through, as vividly as possible, what Jesus would do in each of your situations or activities. (If you don't know what He'd do, perhaps the three principles in Chapter 27 will apply. Also by thinking through what Jesus would do, you'll have your STRATEGY of the Five "S" Mental Approach in Chapter 8.) A variation you might want to try, as you think through what He would do, is to picture Jesus actually in your situations. You'll get better at picturing Him with practice.

3. Then, visualize Jesus asking you, by the Holy Spirit's power, to copy how you just pictured Him going through each of your situations. Remember, you're His personal ambassador and have the responsibility of doing things His way. Mentally picturing Jesus asking you to copy Him will help place emphasis on your responsibility of representing Him.

4. Be determined to accept God's results in each of your situations. And, be ready to thank Him whether the results do or do not turn out the way you desire (1 Thessalonians

5:18). Now, we can easily deceive ourselves into thinking we want to do things Jesus' way. Yet we really want our own predetermined results. This might be as constant a struggle for you as it is for me. We want God's results as long as they work out our way. But, that's wrong, isn't it? God wants us to accept what He permits, or brings our way, as part of His perfect plan. So, it's important that you don't leave your mental preparation session until you're determined to accept God's results, no matter what they are!

One last thing. God wants us to do more than just go through the motions of what Jesus would do. **He's extremely interested in our motives.** We aren't really doing things God's way unless we have Christ-like reasons for doing them. For example, do I fix the leaky faucet my wife has complained about because I know it pleases the Lord when I help her? Or, do I fix it because I don't want her to be annoyed when I watch the football game on TV?

> "...wait until the Lord comes who will both bring to light the things hidden in the darkness and disclose the **motives** of men's hearts; and then each man's **praise** will come to him from God."
>
> 1 Corinthians 4:5

God's praise will come to us based on the purity of our motives in doing things His way. And, you'll have pure motives when you want to do things God's way as an expression of your love for Jesus. Then you're ready to face each of your situations as a personal ambassador for Jesus Christ in more than name only!

FOR INDEPENDENT AND GROUP STUDY

1. Are there any similarities between your life and Hollis' (page 181)?

2. Does Jeremiah 17:9 relate to the way you normally live your Christian life? If it does, give specific illustrations how it relates to your life at home and at work.

3. Give an example, from a recent experience, how things could have been different if you had prepared to represent Jesus Christ in it.

4. How is it possible to prepare for interruptions?

5. What is a benefit from picturing in your mind how Jesus would respond in your situations?

6. Select a situation you face on a regular basis and prepare for it by using the format given in this chapter.

PART FIVE

IN CONCLUSION...

CHAPTER THIRTY-ONE

ONE LAST WORD

"**What would Jesus do now?**" That's the most important question you'll ever ask throughout the day. Hopefully, the information you've read in this book will help you begin to answer that question with more certainity. But, the only authoritative book on knowing exactly what Jesus would do in every situation is the Bible. **It's my desire that, as you now have knowledge of what He'd do in a few of your situations, you'll begin to explore God's word with a new enthusiasm.** Whatever portion you read, ask, "How does this help me follow more closely in the steps of Jesus Christ?" Being committed to follow Him as your Lord might mean refraining from things you're presently doing. Or, it might mean to begin doing many things you're not doing. Following Jesus Christ means we're willing to follow Him regardless of what we normally would like to do in a situation.

Are you willing to stand with the apostle Paul by committing your life to become **an example** of Christ-like living? Paul wrote, "Be imitators of me, just as I also am of Christ" (1 Corinthians 11:1). Although Paul wrote those words to the Corinthian Christians, I'm sure he used the same words to every group of Christians with whom he worked. In fact, we know the Christians in Thessalonica took him up on that challenge. For, He wrote to them, "**You also became imitators of us and of the Lord,** having received the word in much tribulation with the joy of the Holy Spirit, so that **you became an example** to all the believers in Macedonia and Achaia" (1 Thessalonians 1:6-7).

What an impact on other people the Christians in Thessalonica had. The news of their lifestyle spread throughout the entire region. Even in persecution they were committed to follow the example of Paul, and of the Lord, in living the Christian life.

Now, the end of this book all comes down to what you're going to do. **Are you willing to follow in the steps of Jesus Christ so closely, as you're empowered by the Holy Spirit, that other people will say of you, "That person is as close to an example of Jesus Christ as I've ever seen"?** Are you willing to follow Jesus Christ so closely you can say with the apostle Paul, "Be imitators of me, just as I also am of Christ"? My prayers are with you as you pursue your adventure in Christ-likeness.

> "...according to my earnest expectation and hope, that I shall not be put to shame in anything, but that with all boldness, Christ shall even now, as always, be exalted in my body, whether by life or by death. For me, to live is Christ, and to die is gain."
>
> Philippians 1:20-21

PART SIX

TEAR-OUTS

There are 16 pages with dotted lines in the last part of this book. Each has been designed to remind you of an important biblical principle for daily living. Just carefully **tear out** the ones of your choice, **crease them in the center** and stand them in a place where you'll be able to see them regularly (e.g. on the TV, on the dash board of your car, on the bathroom counter, etc.). Then, as you see them, you'll be reminded of God's way of doing things and follow His way instead of your own natural way. By applying what you read, the Holy Spirit will empower you and transform you more into the likeness of Jesus Christ!

Then, when you want to use a focal point on the opposite side of the tear-out page, just reverse your fold, and you're ready to go.

CREATIVE REWARD SYSTEM

Contract

1. Purpose: To help develop Christ-likeness

2. My reward is _____

3. The areas of discipline are:

   A.

   B.

   C.

4. The number of points needed to get my reward are _____

5. Exceptions for not doing my day's disciplines (e.g. sickness, birthdays, etc.):

   A.

   B.

   C.

6. I won't receive my reward until I accumulate the specified number of points.

_____   _____
signature   date

Daily Record

FIRST "S" IS SIGNIFICANCE

THE SIGNIFICANT THING ABOUT EVERY SITUATION IS YOU'RE A PERSONAL AMBASSADOR FOR JESUS CHRIST!

SECOND "S" IS STRATEGY

SINCE YOU'RE CHRIST'S PERSONAL AMBASSADOR IN EVERYTHING YOU DO, IT'S HIGHLY IMPORTANT YOU UNDERSTAND THE STRATEGY OF HOW HE WOULD DO THINGS.

THIRD "S" IS SINGULARITY

EVERY MINUTE OF EVERYTHING YOU DO IS THE SINGLE MOST IMPORTANT MINUTE YOU HAVE BECAUSE YOU'LL NEVER HAVE THAT PARTICULAR MINUTE TO LIVE AGAIN.

FOURTH "S" IS SACRIFICE

SACRIFICE IS COMMITTING YOURSELF TO DO WHAT GOD MOST DESIRES FOR YOU RATHER THAN DOING WHAT YOU MOST DESIRE FOR YOURSELF. IT'S DYING TO WHAT YOU WANT TO DO AND LIVING FOR WHAT JESUS WOULD DO.

FIFTH, "S" IS SOVEREIGNTY

GOD IS SOVEREIGN AND HE EITHER ALLOWS OR CAUSES ALL THINGS TO HAPPEN. IF HE DIDN'T, HE'D BE LESS THAN GOD.

REALIZE THAT GOD WILL USE YOUR CIRCUM-STANCES TO FURTHER HIS PURPOSE AS YOU REMAIN COMMITTED TO HIM AND HIS WAYS.

PHILIPPIANS 1:12

VISUALIZE THE PRESENCE OF JESUS RIGHT NOW.

TAKE EVERY OPPORTUNITY TO LOOK FOR WAYS YOU CAN SERVE OTHERS.

PHILIPPIANS 2:3-4

FOCAL POINT: DIFFERENCE OF AN OPINION WITH A LEADER

CHRIST-LIKE RESPONSE: SHOW RESPECT FOR YOUR LEADER BY GOING TO HIM WITH A POSSIBLE ALTERNATE COURSE OF ACTION, OR REQUEST ONE FROM HIM. THEN, BE SURE YOU LET YOUR LEADER KNOW, BY YOUR ATTITUDE, YOU'LL GO WITH HIS FINAL DECISION.

FOCAL POINT: "UNDESIRABLE" PERSON

CHRIST-LIKE RESPONSE: SEE HIM AS A UNIQUELY DESIGNED INDIVIDUAL. THEN, PERSONALLY INVOLVE YOURSELF TO HELP HIM BLOSSOM INTO THE PERSON GOD INTENDS HIM TO BECOME.

FOCAL POINT: EVERYONE YOU SEE

CHRIST-LIKE RESPONSE: LOOK BEYOND THEIR OUTWARD APPEARANCE TO THE REAL PERSON THEY CAN BECOME IN JESUS CHRIST.

FOCAL POINT: YOUR CONVICTIONS ARE CHALLENGED OR PRESSURED

CHRIST-LIKE RESPONSE: HOLD TRUE TO YOUR CHRIST-LIKE CONVICTIONS, REGARDLESS OF WHAT OTHERS WILL SAY OR THINK, BECAUSE YOUR ONLY RESPONSIBILITY IS TO BE AN AMBASSADOR FOR JESUS CHRIST. AND, YOU'RE TOTALLY ACCEPTED BY HIM!

FOCAL POINT: A PERSON SHOWING AN EMOTIONAL, SPIRITUAL OR PHYSICAL NEED

CHRIST-LIKE RESPONSE: TRY TO MENTALLY AND EMOTIONALLY LOOK INSIDE THE PERSON TO SEE HOW THEY FEEL. TRY TO SEE THINGS FROM THEIR PERSPECTIVE. THEN, IN WORDS, OR ACTION, LET THEM KNOW YOU UNDERSTAND.

FOCAL POINT: FACING A DIFFICULT OR DISCOURAGING SITUATION

CHRIST-LIKE RESPONSE: WHOLEHEARTEDLY PURSUE YOUR TASK, IF IT'S IN LINE WITH GOD'S VALUES, AND REALIZE GOD CAN CAUSE THE SITUATION TO WORK OUT IN YOUR FAVOR IF THAT'S HIS PLAN. THEN, ACCEPT WHATEVER RESULTS COME ABOUT, REALIZING THAT'S WHAT GOD CHOSE TO DO.

FOCAL POINT: WORKING ON A PROJECT

CHRIST-LIKE RESPONSE: TAKE A MOMENT TO DETERMINE HOW YOU CAN BE THE MOST EFFECTIVE IN GETTING YOUR JOB DONE.

FOCAL POINT: A NEED TO KNOW WHAT TO DO

CHRIST-LIKE RESPONSE: EVALUATE WHAT YOU ARE DOING AS TO WHAT HAS THE HIGHEST PRIORITY FOR THAT MOMENT FROM GOD'S PERSPECTIVE.

FOCAL POINT: EMOTION OF ANGER

CHRIST-LIKE RESPONSE: FIRST, SEE YOURSELF AS AN AMBASSADOR FOR JESUS CHRIST IN THE SITUATION. THEN DISCERN THE REASON FOR YOUR ANGER, AND WORK AT SEEING THE SITUATION FROM GOD'S PERSPECTIVE.

FOCAL POINT: PERSON YOU'RE HELPING DOESN'T SHOW ANY APPRECIATION.

CHRIST-LIKE RESPONSE: SINCE REAL GIVING DOESN'T LOOK FOR PAYBACKS, DON'T EXPECT TO BE APPRECIATED. JUST KEEP ON LOOKING FOR WAYS TO HELP.

FOCAL POINT: A NEW DAY

CHRIST-LIKE RESPONSE: AS EACH DAY BEGINS, GO TO A SECLUDED PLACE TO TALK TO GOD ABOUT YOUR DESIRES, CONCERNS AND PRIORITIES FOR THE DAY. THEN, LET HIM TALK TO YOU THROUGH HIS WORD, THE BIBLE.